[redacted]

Leaders of the American Revolution

Betsy Ross

A Flag for a New Nation

Leaders of the American Revolution

Thomas Paine and the Fight for Liberty

John Adams American Patriot

Paul Revere Messenger for Freedom

Betsy Ross A Flag for a New Nation

Benedict Arnold Hero and Traitor

Alexander Hamilton Framer of the Constitution

Molly Pitcher Heroine of the War for Independence

Nathan Hale Courageous Spy

John Paul Jones American Naval Hero

George Washington America's Leader in War and Peace

Leaders of the American Revolution

Betsy Ross

A Flag for a New Nation

Vicki Cox

CHELSEA HOUSE
PUBLISHERS
A Haights Cross Communications Company ®
Philadelphia

CHELSEA HOUSE PUBLISHERS
VP, New Product Development Sally Cheney
Director of Production Kim Shinners
Creative Manager Takeshi Takahashi
Manufacturing Manager Diann Grasse

Staff for Betsy Ross
Executive Editor Lee Marcott
Editorial Assistant Carla Greenberg
Production Editor Bonnie Cohen
Photo Editor Sarah Bloom
Cover and Interior Designer Keith Trego
Layout 21st Century Publishing and Communications, Inc.

A Haights Cross Communications Company ®

www.chelseahouse.com

First Printing

9 8 7 6 5 4 3 2 1

Library of Congress Cataloging-in-Publication Data

Cox, Vicki
Betsy Ross: a flag for a new nation/Vicki Cox
p. cm.—(Leaders of the American Revolution)
Includes bibliographical references and index.
ISBN 0-7910-8618-6 (hardcover)
1. Ross, Betsy, 1752–1836—Juvenile literature. 2. Revolutionaries—United States—Biography—Juvenile literature. 3. United States—History—Revolution, 1775–1783—Flags—Juvenile literature. 4. Flags—United States—History—18th century—Juvenile literature. I. Title. II. Series.
E302.6.R77C69 2005
973.3'092—dc22

2005007536

Contents

OUR RIGHTS AND OUR LIBERTIES

1

The Legend of Betsy Ross

If you know her name, you already know why she is famous. Betsy Ross: creator of the American flag. You may have a picture in your mind of how she made it. Perhaps you imagine that she was sitting by a window or a fireplace; maybe she was sitting in a parlor or a workroom. The flag, with its red and white stripes and its circle of

13 stars on a blue field, is spread across her lap and falls onto the floor. She has a needle in her hand. She wears a frilly cap on her head; her colonial-style dress is decorated with lace on the collar and the sleeves. Perhaps she is alone as she works. Perhaps others are watching her.

Many Americans have heard the story of Betsy Ross and the first American flag. But some scholars believe that the story might better belong in a book of myths and legends, along with George Washington chopping down a cherry tree and Davy Crockett killing a bear when he was three years old.

The story of the first official flag of the not-yet-official United States comes from the story Betsy Ross's grandson told the Philadelphia Historical Society nearly 50 years after she had died. William Canby's story begins at Ross's house at Arch Street and Second Street in Philadelphia, Pennsylvania.

Philadelphia, sometimes called "The City of Brotherly Love," was the second largest city in the English-speaking world. Only London, England's capital, was larger. Philadelphia had built the first American library, firehouse, and

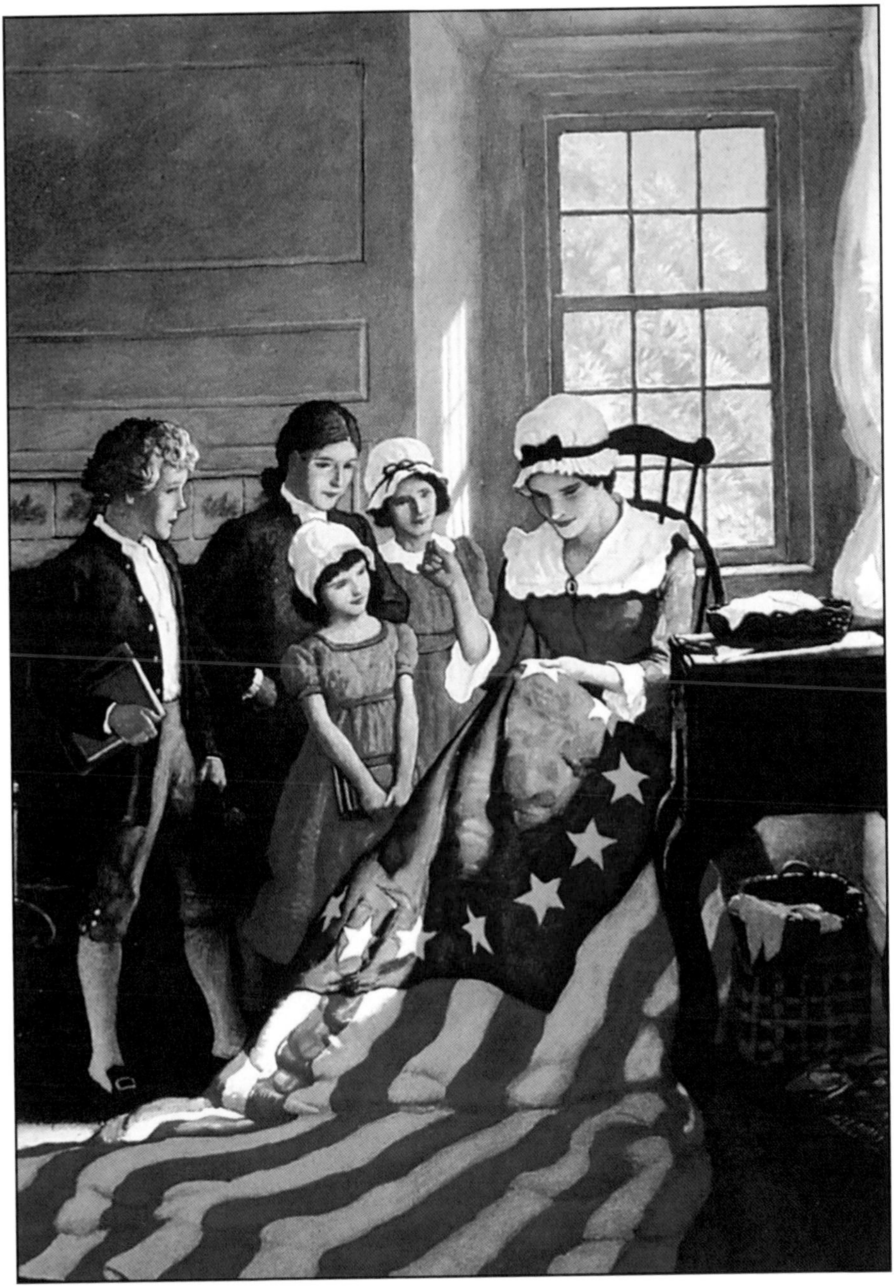

Betsy Ross's creation of the first American flag made her the nation's most famous seamstress.

hospital before Betsy Ross was even born. The streets were lit with whale oil lights and even had sidewalks.

The city was bustling with life. Many shopkeepers conducted business on the first floor of their houses and lived upstairs. Betsy Ross was one of them. Her upholstery shop was well known in the city. Glassmakers, silversmiths, and cabinetmakers had international reputations for their fine work. There were stables, tanneries, lumberyards, and blacksmith shops. Farmers sold livestock, vegetables, fruits, and grains in the marketplace. Taverns drew people who wanted to eat, play cards and chess, or just talk about the day's news. At the docks on the Delaware River, ships unloaded meat, grain, flour, and—more importantly for Betsy Ross—cloth.

In addition to the noise and activity of 40,000 people living their lives, Philadelphia was nearly hysterical with talk of how badly the British government had treated its colonies. Tempers flared as the conversations between Loyalists or Tories (loyal supporters of the policies of the British government) and Patriots or Whigs (those critical of Britain's policies) turned to the possibility of war.

Philadelphia was a bustling center of colonial commerce in the eighteenth century.

A KNOCK AT THE DOOR

According to Ross's grandson, her place in American history began with a knock at the door. She was trying to earn a living by sewing curtains, chair coverings, and clothing. In January 1776, just six months earlier, 24-year-old Betsy Ross had lost her husband, John, in an explosion.

Three gentlemen stood outside the door on that day in May or June (the exact date is uncertain). They came as a secret committee at the order of the Continental Congress. They were to design a new flag that could symbolize a new nation, independent from Great Britain. They wanted Betsy Ross to sew it.

The Second Continental Congress, with 55 delegates from the 13 colonies, was still debating what to do about Britain's treatment of them and its army's attacks on colonial militia. Some of the most important men in all the colonies were gathered there. Betsy Ross surely would have recognized Ben Franklin, the most famous Philadelphian and perhaps the most famous American in the world. Thomas Jefferson, who would write the Declaration of Independence, Samuel Adams and John Hancock, who stirred the rebellion in Boston, and John Adams were, by this time, familiar faces to Philadelphia residents.

The best known of all the delegates would have nearly filled Ross's doorway. At more than six feet tall, George Washington was an impressive man. Under the gold-trimmed, blue and tan uniform, Washington's body was strong. He could ride a horse for seven hours at a time. He could bend a horseshoe with his hands, and crack walnuts between his fingers. His face was sunburned, his eyes were blue-gray, and his face bore tiny scars from smallpox, a disease he had battled as a young man. He covered his hair with a white wig. But it was his dignity and composure that always commanded attention.

Ross would have easily recognized him because they had both attended Christ Church, a few blocks from Ross's home. They may have sat near each other during services. Washington also may have hired her to make shirts for him when he was in Philadelphia.

The second man to tip his hat to her was Colonel George Ross, a well-known businessman. He was a lawyer and politician in Pennsylvania. He and Benjamin Franklin were close friends. Colonel Ross would later fight in the Battle of Trenton (which the colonists won) and the Battles of Germantown and Brandywine outside Philadelphia (which the colonists lost). He was her husband John's uncle.

The third man on Ross's doorstep was Robert Morris. As a delegate to the Congress, he was also a member of another secret committee to find weapons and ammunition for the colonial militia. He had an even more difficult task: finding money to pay for the supplies. He was a good friend of Washington, and the two men would become even closer after Morris found the money for Washington's attack on Trenton, New Jersey, six months after visiting Betsy Ross.

According to Canby's story, the men came with a design for a flag that included 13 alternating red and white stripes. Their flag was square and had 13 six-pointed stars on a blue background in the upper-left corner. The men wanted to know if Betsy Ross could make the flag that they had designed.

Betsy Ross was a Patriot. Her husband, John Ross, had died six months earlier while guarding colonial ammunition. She told the trio, "I've never made one, but I'll try."[1]

A FEW MODIFICATIONS

After agreeing to do the job, Ross supposedly suggested two small changes. First, she suggested making the flag rectangular instead of square, so that it would blow better in the wind. Second, she suggested that the six-pointed stars be changed to five-pointed stars. She claimed that five-pointed stars would be easier to make. Taking a piece of paper, she made several folds and, with a single snip of her scissors, showed them how it could be done. They agreed to her changes and left Ross to her needle and thread.

We don't know when, or if, the committee came back to get the flag. Betsy Ross later said that she gave it to them in late June 1776. We do know that a few days later, on July 4, 1776, the Declaration of Independence was signed, and the struggle to separate from Great Britain officially began.

Service Star Flags

According to legend, Betsy Ross was presented with a design for a flag that included 13 six-pointed stars, one star for each of the colonies. In the story told by Betsy Ross's grandson, Ross then suggested changing the six-pointed stars to stars with five points, a design she supposedly felt was easier to make.

Stars have played a significant role in American flag designs since that time. They have represented colonies and states and, more recently, have been used to represent Americans serving in the military.

The Service Star Banner was first created during World War I, and hung in homes where a family member was serving in the war, a custom that continues to this day. A blue star on the flag represents a family member serving in active duty. A gold star is displayed if a service member has been killed in action or while serving their country.

The first flag of the new nation no longer exists. While there is no real evidence beyond William Canby's story that Betsy Ross actually made the very first flag, there is also no real evidence that proves that she didn't make it.

What does exist is concrete evidence that Betsy Ross lived during one of the most exciting periods of America's history. Not only did she participate in making a new flag at some point; she lived during the making of a completely new nation. The events that we read about in history books went on all around her—on the streets outside her house, and inside her home and her business.

Like the 13 colonies that united to become a country, she thought for herself and stood up for what she believed—no matter what the cost. Her legend aside, the real-life Betsy Ross followed her heart—even if it meant being disowned by her family, friends, and the religion she was raised to believe was correct. Betsy Ross was the perfect person to have made the nation's first official flag.

Test Your Knowledge

1 At the time of the Revolutionary War, London was the largest city in the English-speaking world. What was the second-largest city?

a. Boston.

b. Dublin.

c. Philadelphia.

d. Bombay.

2 Who originally reported that Betsy Ross had made the first American flag?

a. George Washington.

b. Betsy Ross.

c. John Adams.

d. Betsy Ross's grandson.

3 What kind of shop did Betsy Ross own?

a. Silversmith shop.

b. Upholstery shop.

c. Dressmaking shop.

d. Millinery shop.

4 According to legend, which three men formed the "secret committee" charged with creating the first flag?

a. George Washington, George Ross, and Robert Morris.

b. John Ross, Joseph Ashburn, and John Claypoole.

c. George Washington, Thomas Jefferson, and Patrick Henry.

d. John Adams, Thomas Jefferson, and Benjamin Franklin.

5 According to legend, what change did Betsy Ross suggest to the flag's stars?

a. Using 13 stars to represent the colonies, rather than a single star.

b. Changing the six-pointed stars to five-pointed stars.

c. Placing white stars against a blue background, rather than red stars against a white background.

d. Placing the stars in a circle, rather than in two columns.

ANSWERS: 1. c; 2. d; 3. b; 4. a; 5. b

OUR RIGHTS AND OUR LIBERTIES

2

Quaker Family Life

Elizabeth Griscom was born on January 1 in West Jersey, Pennsylvania. She was the eighth of 17 children born in the Griscom family. She arrived the same year that the Liberty Bell arrived in Philadelphia: 1752.

A large part of her life was already determined the minute she took her first breath. Her parents, Samuel

Betsy Ross was born in 1752, the same year that the Liberty Bell arrived in Philadelphia.

Griscom and Rachel James, were Quakers. Their religion set them apart from other colonists. That was the way they wanted it—their own little society within their religious community and within their family.

Quakers lived differently, dressed differently, and even spoke differently from other settlers. They had come to America for religious freedom. In England, they had been jailed, beaten, ridiculed, and had their property taken from them for their beliefs. Their official name was Society of Friends, but they were also called Quakers because they sometimes shook when they thought God was communicating with them.

Their great crusader was William Penn. He fought long and hard for them. His father, an admiral in the British navy, was influential in the king's court. Penn wrote letters and gave speeches to gain some religious freedom for his friends, but he finally decided that the only help for them would be to go to America, where they might practice their faith in safety.

"There is no hope in England," he finally said and asked the king for land where Quakers could live.[2]

For the king's part, granting Penn's request for his "Holy Experiment" cancelled a debt he owed Penn's father and got rid of the Quakers at the same time. He felt that the loss of 45,000 square miles of land was a cheap price to pay.

Because Quakers believed that all people had "Inner Light" or the spirit of God within them, they thought that all people were equal. They called everyone "thee" and "thou," eliminating by this form of address any distinction between classes. They wouldn't tip their hat to anyone or remove it, even in the presence of the king. They wouldn't swear an oath of loyalty to the king. They believed that if they were living the kind of lives they should, their very existence would be truth enough. Obviously, the king took a dim view of these Quaker rules.

Quakers dressed plainly. They wouldn't wear buckles on their shoes, fancy ribbons, gold ornaments, or wigs. They could wear velvet and silk stockings as long as they were for necessity and not just luxury. The Griscom family could not have afforded such expensive clothing.

QUAKER CHILDHOOD

Young Elizabeth quickly gained the nickname Betsy. She dressed much like her mother—in a plain gray dress and bonnet, probably a hand-me-down from one of her six older sisters. Her little brothers would have dressed just like girls until they were old enough to be "breeched," or receive their own pair of britches (pants).

As a Quaker, Betsy could play on a swing, draw on a slate, or cut out paper dolls with scissors. But she could not play with cards. Quakers believed that led to dishonesty. Outdoor games like hide-and-go-seek and tag were allowed, as long as they were played for exercise.

Betsy's brothers could fly kites or sail boats. They were allowed to make pets of squirrels, dogs, or cats. Killing animals for food was acceptable, but hunting for sport was not part of the Quaker way.

Quakers didn't attend plays because actors sometimes spoke against religion. Betsy would not have had storybooks to look at or read. Books, Quakers thought, promoted a world of fantasy and romance instead of encouraging serious study of the Bible.

As a Quaker baby, Betsy could have played with a rattle, but her mother wouldn't have sung her to sleep at night. Quakers thought music provided no intellectual improvement and inspired corrupt thoughts. Instrumental music was forbidden. One newly converted, particularly devout Quaker even refused to whistle.

But playtime, however, was secondary to work. Everyone had to do their share to make sure that the family survived. There were candles to be made, gardens to be tended, wood to be chopped, animals to be fed, and a dozen other things to be done. Betsy would have been put to work early in such a large family. Her mother and sisters would have taught her how to sew, spin, and cook. If other little girls played with cornhusk dolls or wooden dolls, Betsy would have tended her many baby brothers and sisters. There always seemed to be a new one around.

Families were large in Betsy's lifetime. Children often died from diseases like measles or whooping cough that vaccinations have nearly eliminated for us today. Even in Betsy's family, only nine children lived to be adults.

Betsy had to follow strict rules of behavior. Can you imagine living with 17 brothers and sisters and never being able to get angry or raise your voice?

QUAKER WORSHIP

Being quiet was a rule at Quaker meetings, too. Betsy would have gone to a service on First Day (Sunday). Quakers wouldn't use the usual day names because they were named after pagan gods. Betsy's mother and father sat separately on pews, the men and women

Quakers worship in meeting houses—simple buildings without steeples, paintings, or stained-glass windows. This Friends Meeting House, in Philadelphia, is the largest Quaker house of worship in the world.

facing each other. Betsy's older sisters and brothers sat in a special section, or gallery, supervised by one of the group's parents. They weren't supposed to scrape or rub their feet against the floor or seat, bite their nails or stretch, yawn, spit, or draw attention to themselves in any way. If they did break the rules, they were removed from the gallery or whipped.

Everyone sat silently, waiting for someone to stand up and speak the words they thought God had given them to say. It would have been hard for Betsy to keep quiet for two hours during each of Sunday's two services and the one on Fifth Day (or Thursday).

Quakers didn't worship in churches. They believed that they didn't need a fancy place to meet God. They didn't have any of the beautiful decorations other churches had—things like gold ornaments, paintings, or stained glass windows. Their meeting houses were simple, plain buildings without steeples.

Though these ideas might have seemed strange, George Washington admired the Quakers, saying "there is no denomination among us who are more exemplary and useful citizens."[4]

There were more than 50,000 Quakers in America before the Revolution. Most lived in Pennsylvania and Maryland, although others lived as far north as Maine and as far south as Georgia. Betsy's great-grandfather had been one of the early Quaker settlers. Andrew Griscom bought 495 acres of land in 1680, the year after William Penn started his colony. Some of Griscom's land was just outside Philadelphia; some was in the city. Griscom married, started a family, and set up business as a carpenter in Philadelphia.

The city grew. In the middle of the 13 colonies and with easy access to the sea, it became an important trading port. But it also had a touch of the country, too. For several years, animals roamed the streets. A herdsman would blow his horn and all the cattle in town would make their way to him. He would lead them out to the meadow and then, late in the day, he would bring them back into town.

Quakers were pacifists. They didn't want to fight anyone, preferring to find a peaceful solution to conflict. That's where the trouble began. Two years after Betsy was born, her family moved from West Jersey to Philadelphia. But it was no longer a peaceful place. In 1754, the French and Native Americans were fighting Britain for control of land in North America. Quakers who had been in charge of the government resigned over the issue. Others who wanted to fight took over their positions in the city and colony government. In fact, paying for the French and Indian War became a cause of the initial conflict between England and the 13 American colonies.

Betsy grew up in Philadelphia. She was two years old when her family moved there. Betsy's father, Samuel, was a carpenter, like his father and grandfather. He helped build an important building in the city, Carpenters' Hall. He even helped build the

The Flag That First Flew Over the Colonies

Great Britain's flag combined designs from flags created for England and Scotland. England's flag, dating from the Crusades, was a red cross of St. George. When James I of Scotland became king of England in 1603, he brought Scotland's flag with him—a white cross of St. Andrew on a blue field. Because neither the English nor the Scottish would allow their flag to be placed under the other, King James I combined the designs of both flags into a single, new flag in 1606. This flag became known as the Union Flag, symbolizing the union of England and Scotland under a single monarch.

The Union Flag (also called the "Union Jack") was brought to the colonies with the first British settlers in America and this flag flew over the colonies until independence was declared.

bell tower in the Philadelphia State House two years before the new bell arrived from England. It was rung for important announcements. That bell is called the Liberty Bell today, and the building is now called Independence Hall.

Test Your Knowledge

1 Two important events happened in Philadelphia in 1752. One was the birth of Betsy Ross. What was the other?

a. The arrival of the Liberty Bell.
b. The death of William Penn.
c. Benjamin Franklin published the first edition of *Poor Richard's Almanac*.
d. The Quakers built their first meeting house.

2 Why did Quakers come to America?

a. To establish an American branch of the Church of England.
b. To explore a new land.
c. To escape religious persecution in England.
d. To honor a pledge made to William Penn.

3 As a young Quaker girl, what would Betsy Ross have been allowed to do with her free time?

a. Play card games.
b. Play with paper dolls.
c. Play the piano.
d. Read a book of fairy tales.

4 What is a pacifist?

a. A person who believes in freedom of religion.

b. A person who believes in finding a peaceful solution to conflicts.

c. A calming toy given to soothe babies.

d. A person who believed that the colonies should be independent.

5 What building in Philadelphia did Betsy Ross's father help build?

a. The State House.

b. City Hall.

c. William Penn's home.

d. Independence Hall.

ANSWERS: 1. a; 2. c; 3. b; 4. b; 5. d

3

OUR RIGHTS AND OUR LIBERTIES

Growing Up with the Colonies

Education was so important in William Penn's "Holy Experiment" that, for a while, the governor of Pennsylvania introduced public schools. However, as more and more religious groups settled in Pennsylvania, providing schools for everybody proved too much for the government. The Quaker meetings (or groups) took over responsibility for Quaker schools. They believed that children should learn to read and study the Bible so that they would continue in their "plain" lifestyle.

Betsy would have been in school by the time she was seven years old, one of the more than 6,000 school-age Quaker children in Pennsylvania. She was lucky. Not every colonial child was privileged enough to receive a formal education, and few girls ever attended school.

The Philadelphia Yearly Meeting had the largest and best of the schools. Schools in 1741, eleven years before Betsy was born, averaged about 60 students per school. Children could start school any time between the ages of three and fifteen, but most started, like Betsy, at seven and left school by the time they were fourteen. Occasionally, toddlers tagged along with their older brothers and sisters. With so many siblings at home, Betsy might have taken some of the younger ones with her.

Getting an education was serious business. Betsy would have attended school eight hours a day, six days a week. She would have started at 7:00 A.M. in the summer and 8:00 A.M. in the winter. In the morning, she would have concentrated on "book work"—learning to read and write.

In Philadelphia, Betsy could have attended one of four different kinds of schools. She could have gone to a dame school to learn the alphabet, spelling, reading, and how to sew little sayings or the alphabet on cloth. The teacher would have been a woman, who taught children in her kitchen as she did her own work. Betsy might then have progressed to a more advanced school, which offered penmanship (handwriting), French, and math.

The so-called "English school" added lessons in grammar, with rules far more elaborate than those we follow today. Algebra, geometry, geography, and surveying might also have been included.

Only about 40 of the wealthiest and most intelligent Philadelphian boys went to Latin school. Betsy might have been bright enough, but her father was not wealthy enough to pay for her to learn Latin, Greek, arithmetic, accounting, and geography. Besides, a girl would have had little reason to use any of that knowledge.

Textbooks were very demanding. Imagine a kindergartner today learning to read and spell and understand such words as "abolished," "abomination," and "absence."[5] Students didn't learn to read by reading

Some colonial children attended dame schools, where they learned the alphabet, spelling, and reading. Their teacher was often a mother or neighbor who taught children in her kitchen as she did her own work.

simple books. They learned to read by studying words that George Fox, the Quaker founder, wrote: "Christ is the Truth. Christ is the Light. Christ is my Way. Christ is my life. Christ is my Saviour. Christ is my hope of Glory."[6] For variety, they might read the Bible or rules of pronunciation and capitalization. Another option was reading page after page of advice for good living from Fox or other Quaker leaders.

By the time that Betsy finished a Quaker primer (a small book used for teaching young children to read), she would have had a good vocabulary. She could have defined and spelled even more complicated words like "acerbity," "abnegation," and "anathema."[7]

Quaker students were governed by strict rules. They were supposed to talk in the Quaker "plain language" and stay away from children who weren't Quakers. They couldn't call fellow students bad names. It is hard to imagine Betsy being punished at school, but if she had done something wrong, she could have been whipped, slapped on the ear, hit with a rod on the hand, placed in solitary confinement, or had her food taken away from her.

There were limits, however, to how severely the teacher might discipline the students. "No discreet teacher will use broom or mop-stick or door and window-bar to correct their youths; that would be unmanly, as well as unwise, but the rod never hurt, in a skillful hand,"[8] a teaching manual of the time noted.

Betsy's lunchtime would have been two hours long. After it, she would have worked until late afternoon practicing a trade or craft that she "most delightest in."[9] Betsy's Aunt Sarah, who lived with the Griscoms,

Her Quaker faith strongly influenced Ross's early life. Pennsylvania had been founded by William Penn, who negotiated with Native Americans and the king of England to obtain the land where Quakers could settle and freely practice their religion.

may have encouraged Betsy to develop her sewing skills. Early on, Betsy seemed especially talented with a needle and thread. She would have learned more about sewing in her two-hour afternoon sessions. Betsy would have started with making thread, learning to spin flax and wool, knitting gloves and stockings, making hats and baskets out of straw, and embroidery. Her brothers would have learned bookkeeping or a trade like making clocks, watches, shoes, or mathematical instruments.

BECOMING AN APPRENTICE

By the time that she was twelve, Betsy's education was complete. So was her childhood. At home, she was expected to learn to do the things any woman would do in order to run a household. She had to know how to create soap from lye and ashes, cook meals, tend a garden, make herbal remedies, and wash and iron clothing.

While children who had finished school were expected to work, they were still legally children. They might have learned some basic knowledge of a trade in school, but they couldn't transact business in their own names or run a business until they were 21 years old. That's where apprenticeships came in.

Because Philadelphia was such an important seaport, there were as many as 33 different trades that apprentices could learn. There were about 500 apprentices in Philadelphia. Most of these were boys. Luckily for Betsy, her father believed that his daughters should have a skill to support themselves, just like his sons.

Betsy was good at sewing and needlework. In 1765, her father apprenticed her to an upholsterer, John Webster. An upholsterer was someone who manufactured the fabrics and materials used to decorate furniture and rooms. Webster was a well-known tradesman and a Quaker. Under his watchful eye, Betsy learned how to run an upholstery shop. At first, she ran errands and cleaned the shop. Next, she learned small skills until she could sew clothing, quilts, umbrellas, handkerchiefs, curtains, flags, and embroider fabric for furniture.

Being apprenticed to a master tradesman was a long commitment. Betsy would have been apprenticed for seven years to Mr. Webster. The agreement between Betsy's father and Mr. Webster was a formal one. The contract was ripped in half. Mr. Griscom kept one half, and Webster kept the other half. When the apprenticeship was over, Webster was supposed to give his half to Betsy as proof that the apprenticeship was over.

Betsy moved out of her parents' home and went to live with the Websters. The Websters fed her and trained her—with any other apprentices that they were training. Their control over their young charges was nearly absolute. If an apprentice ran away, he or she would be caught, returned to their master, and the apprentice's period of service extended even longer.

Benjamin Franklin had been an apprentice in the printing business. When he lived in Boston, he was apprenticed to his brother, James. He even wrote articles for his brother's newspaper. Franklin didn't like the beatings his brother gave him. After four years, Franklin traveled to Philadelphia and settled there, eventually starting his own printing business. Technically, in the eyes of the law, he was a criminal, having left his brother's service before his seven-year term was ended.

REVOLUTION BEGINS

The flames of revolution sparked in the colonies the year Betsy became an apprentice. In 1763, the French and Indian War ended. It left England with a large debt. The British had been using stamp taxes in England for 50 years, taxing everything from windowpanes and drinks to haircuts. Since the war had taken place in the American colonies, Parliament decided that the colonists should pay for the debt and for the expense of keeping extra troops—about 10,000—in America.

Parliament passed the Sugar Act. It was a variation of a 1733 Molasses Act that the colonists had simply ignored. The Sugar Act taxed sugar, coffee, silks, and herbs from Persia, China, and the East Indies. However, the British Navy was instructed to strictly enforce the new Sugar Act. The colonists were furious at this heavy-handed enforcement.

Samuel Adams wrote, "These unexpected proceedings may be preparatory to new taxations upon us; for if our trade may be taxed, why not our lands? Why not the produce of our lands and everything we possess or make use of?"[10]

Five months later, the British Parliament took control of the colonial currency, decreeing that the colonists could not issue any new money or reprint the old. Parliament also established a Vice Admiralty Court that would rule in favor of the British against smugglers (sometimes colonists themselves). The anger of the colonists grew.

Then, in 1765, England passed the Stamp Act, which required the colonists to pay a tax on 43 items, mostly items printed on paper: wills, contracts, land deeds, property leases, advertisements, calendars, almanacs, newspapers, marriage licenses, diplomas, even playing cards and dice. Supposedly, it was a fair tax, taxing all the people equally.

John Webster, Betsy's master tradesman, would have had to buy paper embossed with a special stamp, paying the tax on any agreements with customers or receipts for work he had done. He also would have paid a tax on any money he received for taking in Betsy and other apprentices.

Passing the Stamp Act was like striking a match in a dry pile of leaves. It angered people in all 13 colonies. The colonists had always governed themselves. Their own assemblies taxed them. With the Stamp Act, Parliament voted to tax the colonists without the colonists voting on the action. The famous phrase "taxation without representation" was born, and peace between England and its 13 colonies became impossible.

Test Your Knowledge

1 What was a dame school?

a. A school for girls.

b. A school that taught students the alphabet, and simple reading and writing.

c. A school that taught Latin, Greek, and geography.

d. A school for apprentices.

2 When she was 14, Betsy Ross became an apprentice. What trade did she learn?

a. How to manage a dressmaking shop.

b. How to manage a flagmaking shop.

c. How to manage an upholstery shop.

d. How to manage a dry goods store.

3 How long was Betsy Ross an apprentice?

a. Six months.

b. One year.

c. Two years.

d. Seven years.

4 The British Parliament passed taxes on the colonies to help pay for what conflict?

a. The Boer War.

b. The Revolutionary War.

c. The French and Indian War.

d. The Spanish-American War.

5 What famous phrase resulted from the Stamp Act?

a. "Taxation without representation."

b. "Don't tread on me."

c. "Give me liberty or give me death."

d. "These are the times that try men's souls."

ANSWERS: 1. b; 2. c; 3. d; 4. c; 5. a

4

A Rebellion in the Colonies

As Quakers, neither Betsy's father nor John Webster would have been part of what happened next. Quakers did not believe in fighting or killing. Some even took care not to prolong the death of a worm while putting it on the fishhook. To violently protest against the Stamp Act would have been against everything they thought important.

Other people, however, were angered to action. In Philadelphia, ringing bells and beating drums brought huge crowds—sometimes as many as 8,000 people—to the State House Yard. A mob threatened the houses of the local stamp collector and the man who appointed him, Benjamin Franklin. A total of 800 men from the carpenter's union guarded their homes. Ship owners hurriedly sent their ships away from Philadelphia before the Stamp Act went into effect. People stopped buying lamb meat so that local herds could produce more wool to make homespun cloth—cloth the colonists intended to use in order to boycott cloth imported from Britain.

Elsewhere, people marched by torchlight, chanting slogans about liberty and eliminating stamps. John Adams wrote, "Our presses have groaned, our pulpits have thundered, our legislatures have resolved, our towns have voted. The Crown officers [those who had supported the Stamp Act] have everywhere trembled, and all their little tools and creatures have been afraid to speak and ashamed to be seen."[11]

In New England, a group called the Sons of Liberty formed. Organized by Samuel Adams, the members included common laborers as well as wealthy lawyers and merchants, united in their protest against what they viewed as unjust taxation. They warned stamp distributors to quit their jobs. The Sons of Liberty hinted that if the stamp distributors continued to enforce the hated tax, they would be tarred and feathered or their houses destroyed. By November 1, 1765, there were no stamp collectors to take charge of the stamped paper. More importantly, colonial merchants gathered at town meetings and agreed to boycott British goods until the Stamp Act was repealed. Philadelphia's 300 merchants supported the boycott more effectively than any of the merchants from any other colony.

British merchants felt the effects of the boycott and pressured Parliament. Their complaints, coupled with colonial violence, persuaded Parliament to repeal the Stamp Act in 1766.

However, Parliament passed the Townshend Duties one year later, attempting to get money from the colonists in another way. The Townshend Duties taxed glass, painter's lead, paper, and tea imported to the colonies. Philadelphians continued to make their own cloth. To obtain the tea they liked so well, they smuggled in Dutch tea rather than buy tea (with its tax) from the British East India Company.

The next year, Britain sent 700 soldiers to Boston, where many rebels lived. Tensions between the Redcoats (a nickname given to British soldiers because of their bright red uniforms) and the locals climaxed on March 5, 1770. An angry mob of Bostonians threatened a group of inexperienced British soldiers, throwing

Tar and Feathering

The Sons of Liberty, and other angry colonial mobs, punished people they didn't like with a coating of tar and feathers. It was actually a horrific practice that could cause severe burns and excruciating pain for the victim.

This is the formula for tar and feathering by a Massachusetts judge, Peter Oliver: "First strip a Person naked, then heat the Tar until it is thin, & pour it upon the naked Flesh, or rub it over with a Tar Brush. . . . After which, sprinkle decently upon the Tar, whilst it is yet warm, as many Feathers as will stick to it. Then hold a lighted Candle to the Feathers, & try to set it all on Fire; if it will burn so much the better. . . . Take also a Halter [a rope with a noose at the end], & put it round the person's Neck, & then cart him to the Rounds [show him around town as an example to others.][*]

* Albert Marrin, *George Washington & the Founding of a Nation* (New York: Dutton, 2001), 88.

rock-filled snowballs and bricks and daring them to fire their weapons. One Redcoat either stumbled or was pushed; his gun discharged. The Redcoats fired into the mob. Five Americans were killed. The Sons of Liberty quickly publicized the "Boston Massacre." Paul Revere's engraving of the event dramatically (and inaccurately) showed soldiers aiming into a crowd of women and children. The picture enraged colonists even more.

FALLING IN LOVE

Meanwhile, back in Philadelphia, Betsy followed her apprenticeship to its conclusion. So did another apprentice, John Ross. In 1773, John Ross opened his own upholstery shop. Betsy worked for him. They became friends, fell in love, and wanted to get married.

For a Quaker, getting married was much more involved than just two people falling in love. The Quaker meeting (group) was very much a part of the process. The couple gave it their certificate "of clearness,"[12] verifying that they were free to marry. Then people from the meeting investigated to see if anyone objected to their marriage and if the individuals were "good Friends" (meaning good and faithful Quakers).[13]

The trouble was that John Ross was not a "good Friend"; he was not a Quaker at all. His father was a minister at Christ Church, an Anglican (or Church of England) church. The Anglicans and the Quakers did not like each other, a result of mistreatment Quakers had suffered at the hands of the Church of England before they had come to America. Betsy had to make a choice—between her faith and her love for John Ross.

Betsy's parents tried to talk her out of the marriage. They could be disciplined by the Quaker meeting for allowing such a "mixed marriage." Representatives from her Quaker meeting talked to Betsy. If they could not convince her to change her mind, she would be cut off from all Quakers, no longer a part of their society. All her Quaker friends would disown her. Even worse, Betsy's mother, father, and her brothers and sisters could not—would not—talk to her either. It was a big price to pay for one man. But Betsy did just that. She was 21 years old and legally of age. She did not give up John Ross.

Even though people sometimes believe colonial women married at a young age, the average age for Quaker women to marry was 22 years and eight months. Betsy was only ten months younger than that. Betsy was not the only Quaker who chose romance over religion. In 1765, about one-third of all Quakers left their religion to marry someone of a different faith.

Even if she had married a Quaker, Betsy would not have had much of a wedding. On the day of the wedding, people arrived at the meeting house and waited in silence. When they felt so moved, the couple stood up and spoke vows they had written themselves. Then, they hosted an elaborate dinner.

Instead, Betsy and John Ross eloped. After working all day, they left Philadelphia after dark. Betsy's sister, Sarah, and her husband helped them get across the mile-wide Delaware River and travel five miles downstream to Glouster, New Jersey. William Hugg, a family friend, found a judge who would perform the wedding. They were married at Hugg's Tavern on November 4, 1773, in front of a huge fireplace—a fireplace that still stands today.

MARRIED LIFE

Betsy and John Ross began their married life facing numerous challenges. Making a living at their upholstery shop was difficult. Neither Betsy's family nor any of the Quaker community that made up a large portion of Philadelphia's population would do business with John, since he was not a Quaker. And a business that dealt with the pretty "extras" of living seemed frivolous at a time that war seemed near.

The Quaker society gave Betsy several chances to admit her "mistake." But she did not think she had made one. Finally, on May 24, 1774, she was "read out of Meeting."[14] Records show "Elizabeth Ross, late Griscom . . . having had her Education and made profession with us the People called Quakers . . . hath disunited herself from the Religious Fellowship with us."[15]

The Rosses worshiped at John's father's church. Christ Church was an impressive building, one of the largest in the entire 13 colonies. The tall steeple pierced the sky. Church services had music, singing, a minister who preached sermons, and lovely decorations—things Betsy had never enjoyed in Quaker services.

Things were not so lovely in the colonies. Eventually, Parliament repealed the taxes that had so enraged the colonists. But King George III, to help out the financially struggling British East

India Company, decreed that the colonists could buy tea only from it and that they would pay a tax of three cents per pound on the tea. It was a small tax, but it seemed, to the angry colonists, to symbolize that the king had a right to tax anything in their lives without them being able to speak for themselves.

Again, crowds gathered at Philadelphia's State House. Mobs persuaded merchants not to accept the taxed British tea. An anonymous writer warned in the *Pennsylvania Packet* newspaper that any tea stored in warehouses might meet with "trifling accidents."[16] A "Committee for Tarring and Feathering" warned ship pilots what might happen to them if they brought a tea ship into port.[17] The Boston Tea Party might just have easily taken place in Philadelphia, or in any other colonial city.

New York refused to allow the tea to be brought ashore. In Charleston, South Carolina, officials allowed tea to be unloaded, but the tea was then left to rot in warehouses. But it was in Boston that events came to a crisis, when three tea ships—the *Dartmouth*, the *Beaver* and the *Eleanor*—tied up to Griffin's Wharf for two weeks. On December 16, 1773, members of the Sons of Liberty launched the Boston Tea Party.

Dissatisfaction with British policies erupted throughout the colonies. In Massachusetts, the tax on tea prompted the Boston Tea Party.

Townspeople, who were by day silversmiths, merchants, bakers, farmers, and wharf workers, became Mohawk Indians. Though they blackened their faces and threw blankets over themselves, they did not act like they were on the warpath. They did not sneak up under cover of darkness and attack.

"Everything was as light as day, but the means of lamps and torches—a pin might be seen lying on the wharf,"[18] said Robert Sessions, one of the men who disguised themselves that night.

The men boarded the three ships. George Robert Twelves Hewes remembered, "We were then ordered by our commander to open the hatches, and take out all the chests of tea and throw them overboard, and we immediately proceeded to execute his orders; first cutting and splitting the chests with our tomahawks so as thoroughly to expose them to the effects of the water."[19]

They disturbed nothing except the 342 chests of tea leaves. More than a thousand people watched while the Mohawks "made a teapot of the harbor" with British tea that would be valued today at a million dollars.[20] Even British Admiral John Montague watched. He shouted to the crowd as it left, "Well boys, you have had a fine, pleasant evening for your Indian caper—haven't you. But mind, you've got to pay the fiddler yet."[21]A song in the taverns publicized the event: "Rally, Mohawks! bring out your axes, And tell King George we'll pay no taxes, On his foreign tea."[22]

Parliament came down with a heavy fist on rebellious Boston with the Coercive Acts. Colonists had a different name for them: The Intolerable Acts.

English ships closed Boston Harbor, vowing to keep it closed until the colonists had repaid the cost of the ruined tea. Parliament suspended the powers of the Massachusetts government. Anyone who opposed the Acts could be arrested and tried for sedition (rebellion against the British government). The military appointed local officials. Americans, charged with certain crimes, could be shipped to England, where they would have little chance of a fair trial. Under General Thomas Gage, 4,000 British Redcoats—one for every Bostonian male—arrived in Boston.

The soldiers moved into the homes of Boston citizens. Everything stopped in Boston. People did not work. They earned no money. They couldn't buy food. But the Bostonians were determined not to pay for the tea. The British were determined that they would. "We must control them or submit to them," said the British prime minister.[23]

Test Your Knowledge

1 Why did angry mobs threaten the home of Benjamin Franklin after passage of the Stamp Act?

a. Franklin believed that the Stamp Act was a fair and just tax.
b. Franklin was known to be a supporter of British Parliament and King George III.
c. Franklin had appointed the local stamp tax collector.
d. Franklin had published an editorial critical of the Sons of Liberty.

2 Who was John Ross?

a. Betsy Ross's father.
b. Betsy Ross's husband.
c. Betsy Ross's employer.
d. Betsy Ross's brother.

3 Why did Betsy's parents not want her to get married?

a. The man she loved was not a Quaker.
b. They thought she was too young.
c. They thought she should marry someone wealthier and more successful.
d. They wanted her to finish her apprenticeship first.

4 Why didn't members of the Quaker community shop at the Ross upholstery shop?

a. They believed that upholstery was frivolous and not suited to their "plain" lifestyle.
b. Most Quakers did not have the money to afford luxury items.
c. They did not want to pay the heavy taxes on fine fabrics.
d. They did not want to shop at a business owned by a non-Quaker.

5 How was Christ Church different from the Quaker meeting houses Betsy had attended as a child?

a. It had a steeple.
b. There was singing during the services.
c. The minister preached a sermon during the services.
d. All of the above.

ANSWERS: 1. c; 2. b; 3. a; 4. d; 5. d

5

OUR RIGHTS AND OUR LIBERTIES

A Time of War

On May 19, 1774, Paul Revere rode to Philadelphia, asking for help for Boston. Though Boston was about 300 miles away, Philadelphians had heard of the hardships Bostonians were suffering under the Intolerable Acts and were outraged. So were people in the other colonies. If the British could do such things to British citizens in

Massachusetts, they asked, what would keep them from sending in troops and closing down the local governments in all the colonies? Philadelphians sent flour to the besieged Bostonians. South Carolina sent money and rice; Long Islanders sent sheep.

On September 5, 1774, representatives from nearly all of the colonies met in Philadelphia in Carpenters' Hall—one of the structures Betsy Ross's father helped to build. In a white-paneled room, the men worked from 9:00 A.M. until 3:00 P.M. They stopped for fine dinners and rich red wines. They met again until 6:00 or 7:00 P.M., going over the discussions.

A total of 56 delegates from 12 colonies debated their options. Not wanting to anger England, Georgia did not send any delegates. The colony needed British soldiers to help in ongoing battles against Native Americans.

The other colonies did not want independence—yet. They simply wanted to be treated fairly. They wanted their rights as Englishmen to be honored. They wanted the British army to stop policing their streets and occupying their homes. They continued the boycott of all goods coming from England to the colonies, and they refused to sell anything to England.

Betsy and John Ross immediately felt the effect of the boycott. They depended on imports of fine fabrics to make the drapes, cushions, and covered furniture people came to their shop to buy. Without those fabrics, they struggled to make a living.

The colonial delegates called themselves the Continental Congress. They sent a petition to King George III. "Permit us to be as free as yourselves," they wrote, "and we shall ever esteem a union with you to be our greatest glory and our greatest happiness."[24]

While they wrote of peace, they also talked among themselves of war. Some delegates favored neither compromising with Parliament nor becoming independent. The colonists themselves were divided. Some colonists formed militia companies, and called themselves Minutemen. Loyalists supported the king. The rest were undecided, waiting to see which side would win out. The delegates ended their meeting on October 24, agreeing to meet again in May 1775, if their complaints were not addressed.

THE FIRST BATTLES

On April 24, 1775, a month before the Second Continental Congress was to meet again, Betsy and

John Ross—and all of Philadelphia—learned about the Battles of Lexington and Concord. Few realized it, but these battles in Massachusetts marked the beginning of the Revolutionary War.

The conflict began because the British general, Thomas Gage, was looking for two leaders of the rebellion in Massachusetts, John Hancock and Samuel Adams. He discovered that they were hiding in Lexington, about 15 miles from Boston. Hancock was a wealthy and refined Boston merchant whose money helped the cause for independence. He had even funded his own militia, the Boston Cadets. Samuel Adams had no money and cared nothing about appearances. But he was passionate about independence. His letters and editorials in newspapers were inspiring people to consider action against the British authorities. Gage believed that if he could capture these two leaders, he could cripple the rebellion. He also learned that the colonists were hiding 100 barrels of gunpowder and 14 cannon in Concord. He wanted those prizes, as well.

The colonists discovered Gage's plan, but didn't know if the British would start out for Lexington by land or sea. Signals from the Old North Church—

lanterns in the steeple—set Paul Revere and William Dawes on their way to spread the news.

"I alarumed almost every house—shouting 'The regulars are out!'—till I got to Lexington," Revere said later.[25]

Paul Revere's famous midnight ride enabled Adams and Hancock to escape. He warned Lexington Minutemen in time for them to prepare for the approaching Redcoats. Still, the colonists were greatly outnumbered. About 80 Minutemen with guns, hatchets, and bayonets waited to stop 800 Redcoats. The British commander, Major Pitcairn, ordered his troops not to fire and yelled to the colonists, "Disperse ye villains, ye rebels! Disperse! lay down your arms! why don't you lay down your arms and disperse?"[26]

A shot from behind a stone wall or from a window started it all. No one knows who fired the first shot. Both the British and the Minutemen later claimed that it had come from the other side. In the ten-minute gunfire that followed, eight Americans died and ten were wounded; the rest scattered. Proclaiming their victory, the British marched five miles down the road toward Concord, shooting their guns in the air and beating their drums.

Forewarned, Concord residents had been busy the night before hiding their weapons and ammunition. A cannon was buried in a plowed field; church silver

A Land of Many Flags

Before the colonies were unified under a single flag, different flags represented regions, regiments, or particular militias. The pine tree was often used in New England flags. Sometimes it was placed in the corner of a white canton that was divided by St. George's cross. The rest of the flag was red. A design that enlarged the pine tree over the entire canton may have flown at the Battle of Bunker Hill in 1775. New England ships commanded to board British merchant ships carrying ammunition and weapons needed a flag to identify themselves to each other and to show others they were not pirates. Their flag had a pine tree in the center and the words "Appeal to Heaven" or "An Appeal to Heaven" above or below it.

A popular flag design from the South included the rattlesnake. One early flag was known as the Gadsden flag. A rattlesnake, coiled and ready to strike, was centered on a yellow background. The motto "Don't Tread on Me" was printed below. Esek Hopkins, commander of the new Continental fleet, set to sea for the first time under this flag in February 1776.

was hidden in a barrel of soap. From a hill outside Concord, the militia watched the British advance. The alarm had spread through other counties. Women threw bread, beef, and stockings in pillowcases and gave them to their husbands as they left. Seeing smoke rise, the Concord Minutemen believed that the British were burning their homes and headed into town. Approximately 500 Minutemen advanced towards the North Bridge. Once again, neither a British nor a colonial officer gave the command to fire, but five minutes later, Minutemen and Redcoats both lay dead.

The British were shocked that their enemies were such good shots. They withdrew. They fled to Boston, with 3,000 militia—who had hurried in from outlying farms and villages—firing at them from behind trees, fences and bushes, over hedges and out windows. "We began to run rather than retreat in order," one British officer said.[27]

Outnumbered two to one, the British lost 272 of their 1,800 soldiers. The colonists felt a sudden surge of hope and pride. They had stood up to the mighty British Army and won. One British officer said, "Whoever dares to look at them as an irregular mob, will find himself much mistaken. They have men amongst them who know very well what they are about."[28]

CREATING AN ARMY

A month later, on May 10, the Second Continental Congress reconvened in Philadelphia at the State House. Some delegates, like Benjamin Franklin, wanted independence. Others wanted to settle their differences with England peacefully. They sent an "Olive Branch Petition" to England, proposing that if colonial legislatures were made equal to Parliament they would remain loyal to the king. The king responded by sending 20,000 more troops to the colonies. Things were rapidly coming to a climax.

On June 14, the Second Continental Congress voted to do something important: create the Continental Army. Until the battles of Lexington and Concord, groups of unorganized militia volunteers milled about the country. Some 10,000 of them had camped outside Boston, surrounding British forces there. Massachusetts wanted someone to take charge of them.

The next day, John Adams nominated George Washington to be the commander-in-chief of the new

The Second Continental Congress, meeting at Philadelphia's State House in 1775, nominated George Washington to serve as commander-in-chief of the Continental Army.

army. Embarrassed, Washington blushed and walked out of the room. But others agreed with Adams. A Connecticut delegate said that Washington was "no harum-scarum, ranting, swearing, fellow but sober, steady and calm."[29] He was the best choice. He had commanded a militia. Years before, he had fought in the French and Indian War. He supported the cause of independence. He was a Virginian. The colonies would look united if the New England men were commanded by a man from the South. Washington humbly accepted, saying, "I this day declare with the utmost sincerity that I do not think myself equal to the command I am honored with."[30]

Before Washington could assume command of his troops in Massachusetts, a major battle developed. Today, we remember it as the Battle of Bunker Hill, but it actually took place on Breed's Hill.

Word spread that the British were planning to come out of Boston for a major assault. With muffled shovels and in the moonlight, 900 colonists fortified Breed's Hill with trenches and dirt walls reaching five to six feet high. With its long sides and high walls, it looked like a fort. General Gage, seeing the militia commander scurry about in the distance, asked his aide, Abijah Willard, about him. The officer was Willard's brother-in-law, William Prescott.

"Will he fight?" Gage asked.

"I cannot answer for his men," Willard said, "but Prescott will fight you to the gates of hell."[31]

The British would soon learn where that location might be. Classical European fighters, they intended to march straight at the earthen fort, forcing the colonists to turn and run. Their leader, General Howe, told his

2,200 troops before the battle, "I do not in the least doubt that you will behave like Englishmen and as becometh good soldiers."[32]

The afternoon of June 16, the Minutemen had more than enough courage, but were lacking in guns and ammunition. They had melted down the organ pipes in Christ Church for bullets. Some men loaded their guns with nails and pieces of iron.

The British marched towards the fort in long, straight lines. The colonists waited, instructed by one of their officers, "Don't fire until you see the whites of their eyes."[33] When the British were about a hundred feet away, the colonists fired. Redcoats fell dead everywhere.

The British retreated to the bottom of the hill and tried again, stepping over the bodies of their dead. The colonists waited until they were 50 feet away, then fired again. More British staggered and died. Confused, the Redcoats ran for cover. Their officers rallied them for a third charge. The colonists waited until they were 20 feet away and fired the last of their ammunition. This time, the British did not retreat.

The colonists fought with rocks and their fists, but were no match for the two-foot-long bayonets the

According to Betsy Ross, she met with George Washington, Robert Morris, and George Ross in mid-1776, and was then asked to design a new flag for America.

British carried. The British took Breed's Hill and Bunker Hill behind it. A total of 500 Americans and 1,000 British soldiers lay dead. "The dead lay as thick as sheep in a fold," a participant said.[34]

Though the battle was technically won by the professional British soldiers, it was a moral victory for the militia of farmers, merchants, tradesmen, blacksmiths, and bakers. As Nathanael Greene later said, "I wish we could sell them another hill at the same price."[35]

Washington left Philadelphia, escorted by one of the city's militia, to join an army that had no country. John and Betsy Ross may have been among the crowd of Philadelphians that watched him depart. They were Patriots and supported the cause for which Washington and his men would fight. John Ross would later do his part, guarding Philadelphia.

Test Your Knowledge

1. One colony did not participate in the First Continental Congress. Which one?
   a. New York.
   b. Pennsylvania.
   c. Delaware.
   d. Georgia.

2. Why did the boycott of English goods impact the Ross upholstery shop?
   a. They needed the imported English fabrics to make drapes, curtains, and furniture coverings.
   b. They wanted to be able to serve tea to customers.
   c. They wanted to be able to export their drapes and curtains to England.
   d. None of the above.

3. Which battle or battles marked the start of the Revolutionary War?
   a. The Battle of Bunker Hill.
   b. The Battles at Lexington and Concord.
   c. The Battle of Trenton.
   d. The Battle of Saratoga.

4. Who nominated George Washington to be commander-in-chief of the Continental Army?

a. George Ross.

b. Benjamin Franklin.

c. John Adams.

d. Thomas Jefferson.

5. What was the "Olive Branch Petition"?

a. A proposal that if colonial legislatures were made equal to Parliament, they would remain loyal to the king.

b. A proposal to disband the colonial militias if British troops would leave Boston.

c. A proposal to send a peace delegation to negotiate with the British general in charge of the forces in America.

d. A proposal to create a unified army with George Washington as its commander-in-chief.

ANSWERS: 1. d; 2. a; 3. b; 4. c; 5. a

6

OUR RIGHTS AND OUR LIBERTIES

Betsy Ross and the Founding Fathers

Washington arrived in Cambridge, Massachusetts, on July 2, 1775. If he expected to find an army, he was in for a surprise. He later wrote that 15,000 "exceedingly dirty and nasty people" waited for him.[36] They could shoot a gun, but were barely trained, badly disciplined, and sadly equipped. They wouldn't take orders, take a bath, or relieve themselves in private. They enlisted for just six months at a time.

Washington set about to make them into the Continental Army. His rules were strict and clear. No gambling, drinking, fighting. Everyone had to shave, change their clothes twice a week, and use latrines (specific areas designated as outdoor toilets). He had no patience with those who broke the rules. Washington wanted to punish offenders with 500 lashes, but was limited to 100. Once, he jumped a fence and rode into the middle of a brawl, grabbing two soldiers who were fighting, lifting them off the ground, and shaking them.

Back in Philadelphia, the delegates of the Second Continental Congress discussed how the colonies should proceed. The Philadelphia militia trained on High Street and Chestnut Street, their drums beating the rhythm. Betsy and John Ross would have heard them practicing.

After Esek Hopkins had sailed to the Bahamas and stolen a large quantity of powder, guns, and a hundred cannons, the militia had a large responsibility. Some of Hopkins's prizes were hustled off to Washington's headquarters, but the rest were warehoused along Philadelphia's waterfront.

With a large Tory (or Loyalist) population in Philadelphia, such valuable supplies could have been targeted for sabotage. As the largest city in the colonies and the location of the Second Continental Congress, Philadelphia was a prime British target. John Ross joined the militia and volunteered to guard the ammunition warehouse.

On Betsy's twenty-fourth birthday—January 1, 1776—two important events occurred. First, an explosion ignited the ammunition stored on the waterfront. John Ross was badly hurt. For three weeks, Betsy tried vainly to help her husband recover. Sadly, he died on January 21, 1776, and was buried in the Christ Church Cemetery, the first casualty of war in the congregation. Second, Washington ordered a flag to be raised over his headquarters near Boston. The Grand Union Flag, with the crosses of St. George and St. Andrew in the canton, looked like a distant relative of Great Britain's flag. British soldiers who saw it, even with its 13 red and white stripes, thought that Washington was signaling his surrender. They were wrong.

On January 9, 1776, Thomas Paine's *Common Sense* was published in Philadelphia. From the moment it appeared, everyone who could read wanted to read it. Betsy would have been among them. Those who couldn't read wanted it read to them. In plain language the average person could understand, Paine spelled out the arguments for declaring independence.

"Everything that is right or natural pleads for separation. The blood of the slain, the weeping voice of nature cries, 'TIS TIME TO PART,'" he wrote. "Even the distance at which the Almighty hath placed England and America, is a strong and natural proof, that the authority of the one, over the other, was never the design of Heaven. . . ."[37]

The book was tremendously popular, selling over 100,000 copies in three months. By the end of the war, it had sold 500,000 copies. More than the battles taking

The Grand Union Flag

The Grand Union Flag was so similar to England's official flag that British soldiers thought that the colonists were surrendering when they first saw it hoisted at Washington's Cambridge headquarters on January 1, 1776. Six white horizontal stripes on a red background created 13 stripes. A small Union Jack (with the crosses of St. Andrew and St. George) was in the corner.

place in distant Massachusetts, *Common Sense* inspired people towards independence.

In the meantime, Washington solved the stalemate between the British trapped in Boston and his troops surrounding them. Cannons powerful enough to shell the town were hauled in by oxen from 300 miles away. The troops built fortifications overnight at Dorchester Heights and had their guns in place by daybreak on March 4.

"My God! These fellows have done more work in one night than I could make my army do in three months," General William Howe said when he saw what they had done.[38] He knew that the cannon would turn any battle into a slaughter.

Howe offered to leave Boston without harming the population if Washington would not fire on his British troops. Washington agreed. Incredibly, Washington's untrained army won the standoff without firing a shot. A total of 170 British ships left the harbor for Canada.

THE DELEGATES DEBATE

Washington returned to Philadelphia. There, the delegates were still debating. Each morning they made their way to the State House. Living just a few blocks

Betsy Ross's home offers visitors insight into life in Philadelphia in the eighteenth century.

away, Betsy could have easily recognized them. Betsy would have already known Ben Franklin, a Philadelphia resident. He was the best-known person in all the colonies. Wearing the bifocals he invented, he was the oldest of the delegates.

It didn't take people long to recognize John Hancock. He rode around town in a carriage with 25 servants in front of him and 25 trailing behind him. His silk stockings, lace, satin, and brocades were evidence of his great wealth.

Fiery Samuel Adams was Hancock's complete opposite. He cared nothing for fashion, looking like he had slept in his clothes the night before. His Boston friends had bought him a new red suit, shoes, and silver buckles before he arrived in Philadelphia, hoping to make him look a bit more presentable.

Thomas Jefferson of Virginia was a quiet, tall, slim, redhead who rented rooms near the edge of town. "During the whole time I sat with him in the Congress, I never heard him utter three sentences together," John Adams said.[39]

John Adams, a Boston lawyer, hurried everywhere. In four years, he served on 90 Continental Congress committees, chairing 24 of them. With Congress in session nearly all day, Betsy and others would have seen this short, plump, balding man hustling to breakfast meetings before 6:00 A.M.

All these men favored independence. But not all the delegates or the colonies they represented did. Pennsylvania's legislature had instructed its delegates to vote against it.

Every day, the delegates gathered at the State House and waited for the signal to enter—the ringing of a hand bell. Though they might not agree on separating from Great Britain, they agreed that no one should know the details of their arguments. Once they entered the assembly room, the door was locked behind them. The windows were closed to keep people passing by from hearing what was being discussed. It must have been miserable in there in the summer's sultry heat. Horseflies flew into the small openings, biting the delegates on the back of their hands and necks.

Later, historians would uncover some information in the diaries of the delegates about the heated debates and arguments. John Adams, the future president of the United States, once jumped on his desk and threw his wig at those who disagreed with him.

Finally, on June 7, 1776, a delegate from Virginia, Richard Lee, offered a resolution that stated, "That these United colonies are, and of a right out to be, free and independent States, that they are absolved from all allegiance to the British Crown and that all political connection between them and the State of Great Britain is, and ought to be, totally dissolved."[40]

When the delegates were polled to see how they'd vote, only seven colonies favored independence—a majority, but only by one vote. Something as important as declaring independence needed to be decided with more votes than that. "Some among us urge strongly for Independence and eternal separation," a North Carolina delegate noted, "while others wish to wait a little longer and to have the opinion of their constituents."[41] Congress recessed for three weeks—until July 1, 1776.

Before it recessed, Congress appointed a committee of five to work on a declaration of independence—in case it might be needed. Bostonian John Adams, Roger Sherman of Connecticut, Ben Franklin, Robert Livingston of New York, and Thomas Jefferson made up the group.

Adams, one of the most talkative of the delegates, would have been the logical choice to write the declaration of independence. But Adams told Jefferson to write the declaration. "Reason first—You are a Virginian and a Virginian ought to appear at the head of this business. Reason second—I am obnoxious, suspected and unpopular. You are very much otherwise. Reason third—You can write ten times better than I can."[42]

Jefferson had just two and a half weeks to write the declaration. He was staying at Market Street and Seventh Street across from a stable. Jefferson could look out the window of his two-room apartment and see open fields. He wrote on a portable desk he had designed himself, a sort of colonial laptop. Adams and Franklin made changes to his draft of the declaration before giving it to Congress on June 28, 1776.

It was during this time—between May and June 1776, with pro-independence delegates arguing with anti-independence delegates about forming a new country and with the British about to attack in New York—that Betsy Ross claims George Washington, commander-in-chief of the army, Robert Morris, and George Ross came to her shop and asked her to make a new flag.

Test Your Knowledge

1. What assignment did John Ross accept to help the Patriot cause?
   a. He guarded the State House while the Continental Congress was in session.
   b. He patrolled the streets of Philadelphia, spying on Loyalists.
   c. He traveled to Massachusetts to serve with Washington.
   d. He guarded the ammunition warehouse.

2. How did John Ross die?
   a. He was killed in battle.
   b. He was wounded in an explosion and did not recover.
   c. He was infected with yellow fever.
   d. He was shot in a duel.

3. What was the title of Thomas Paine's popular pamphlet that spelled out the arguments for independence?
   a. *Now is the Time.*
   b. *The Struggle for Liberty.*
   c. *Common Sense.*
   d. *The Federalist Papers.*

4 Which wealthy delegate rode around Philadelphia in an elegant carriage, with 25 servants in front of him and 25 servants behind him?

a. Thomas Jefferson.

b. Benjamin Franklin.

c. John Adams.

d. John Hancock.

5 Why did John Adams believe that Thomas Jefferson should be the author of the Declaration of Independence?

a. Because Jefferson was from Virginia.

b. Because Jefferson was a better writer than Adams.

c. Because Jefferson was more popular than Adams.

d. All of the above.

ANSWERS: 1. d; 2. b; 3. c; 4. d; 5. d

7

A New Nation

Philadelphia was again abuzz. Betsy Ross and other Philadelphians watched as the Second Continental Congressional delegates rode back into town on horseback and in carriages.

The delegates milled about outside the State House until the business of the day began. The delegates were an argumentative bunch, strong of opinions and loyal to differing religions, regions, and politics. The delegations varied in size. A majority vote within each group determined the colony's one vote on any issue. New England favored independence; the southern colonies leaned towards it. The middle colonies would determine the outcome; Pennsylvania was crucial.

On July 1, the delegates resumed their meetings. They had to talk above the noise of a summer storm. Speeches from both sides warmed the already hot room. Unofficially, nine colonies had come to favor independence. Pennsylvania and North Carolina opposed it. Delaware's delegates were divided, and the New York delegation waited on instructions from home. The vote had to be more decisive than that.

Someone moved that the vote be postponed for one day. Then, they read a depressing letter from Washington, who reported events in New York. "For two or three days past three or four ships have been dropping in and I just now received an express . . . that forty five arrived today, some say more, and I suppose the whole fleet will be within a day or two. I am hopeful before they are prepared to attack, that I shall get some reinforcements. . . ."[43]

The next day, the delegates heard another depressing letter from Washington about British forces: "I had only been informed of the arrival of Forty Five of the Fleet in the morning; since that I have received Authentic Intelligence . . . that one hundred and ten sail came in before Night . . . and that more were seen about dusk in the offing."[44]

With the British poised to attack, the time for voting—one way or the other—was upon them. A Delaware delegate whose vote would swing Delaware towards independence was absent. When he arrived, mud-spattered and exhausted from an 80–mile ride from Dover, the voting began. Two Pennsylvania delegates, John Dickinson and Robert Morris (one of the secret visitors to Betsy Ross), both opposed independence. They did not come to the meeting. Without them, the Pennsylvania delegation could change its vote for independence. The voting didn't take long, and the result was 12 votes for independence. New York's delegation didn't vote, unsure what their legislature preferred.

A DECLARATION OF LIBERTY

The next step was to declare America's independence.

Surprisingly, reading through Thomas Jefferson's rough draft was not a top priority for the Congress over the next two days. They mulled over letters, new commissions, and instructions to various committees while the Declaration lay on the clerk's desk.

Finally, Congress read Jefferson's Declaration. They examined words, phrases, and paragraphs throughout the afternoon of July 3, throwing out some words, rearranging phrases, and shredding paragraphs. Jefferson sat in the back of the room, taking in all the criticism.

July 4 was a clear day, full of sunshine. Thomas Jefferson managed to buy a new thermometer and nine pairs of gloves for his wife before the 9:00 A.M. session started. Again, he sat with his portable desk on his knees, taking notes as the Congress went through the Declaration.

Congress threw out entire paragraphs where Jefferson blamed King George III for the slave trade. John Adams passionately argued for preserving each word, defending Jefferson's document against numerous edits and amendments. In all, the Congress made 86 changes, reducing Jefferson's thoughts to 1,337 words. Then the delegates approved the Declaration of Independence.

No bells rang; no gun salutes were fired. The Congress simply directed that copies of the Declaration should go to the colonial legislatures and to the army's commanding officers. Then Congress went on with other routine business, like hiring a new private secretary, electing Indian affairs commissioners, and ordering that flint belonging to the army be delivered to General Washington.

John Adams recognized the Declaration's importance. He wrote his wife, "It ought to be solemnized with pomp and parade, with shows, games, sports, guns, bells, bonfires, and illuminations from one end of this continent to the other, from this time forward forever more."[45]

On July 8, the 2,000-pound State House bell rang from its belfry. Chimes pealed from the Christ Church spire for an hour. People all over Philadelphia hurried into the grassless area outside the building. Betsy Ross would have walked four blocks from her house to be among them for such an important announcement.

Christopher Marshall, a Congressman said, "[We] went in a body to the State House Yard, where in the presence of a great concourse [group] of people, the Declaration of Independence was read by John

Nixon. . . . There were bonfires, ringing bells, and other demonstrations of joy upon the unanimity and agreement of the Declaration."[46]

The news traveled throughout the colonies. People cheered; more bells rang. Men fired their rifles and muskets. More people lit bonfires and burned or hung symbols of King George III. The Sons of Liberty, Samuel Adams's civilian gang, pulled down a large statue of King George. It was melted down and was later made into 42,088 bullets. The same day, the New York State convention, having read the Declaration, sent word to its delegates in Philadelphia to vote for independence. That made the vote unanimous. On July 9, Washington had the Declaration read to the troops.

Usually, only the president of the Congress, in this case John Hancock, signed such paperwork. But someone had proposed that every member of the Congress sign the Declaration—perhaps to show that all colonies were in agreement. On August 2, 56 men added their signature to the document. Nine members of the Pennsylvania delegation signed—including Robert Morris, George Ross, and Benjamin Franklin. Morris had not wanted independence, and Ross, a newcomer to the delegation, had not voted at all.

John Hancock, serving as president of the Continental Congress, signed the Declaration of Independence with a large and bold signature, so that his name could be clearly read.

Lawyers, doctors, clergymen, farmers, and plantation owners were among the signers. George Washington was in New York and did not sign.

In December, fearing Philadelphia's capture, Congress packed up the Declaration and other papers and fled to Baltimore for two months.[47] Betsy Ross did not have that option. She was one of many Philadelphians who stayed in their city. The city was put under martial law and shops were closed. Betsy Ross found earning a living even more difficult.

DESPERATE TIMES

In August 1776, Britain's mighty navy and army were ready for a major attack. New York's harbor was filled with British ships; General Howe had 32,000 men, including 8,000 hired Hessian soldiers from Germany. Facing them were Washington's 28,000 men; only about 19,000 were trained.

Not surprisingly, Washington was defeated. Instead of fighting from behind houses and trees as the militias had successfully done at Lexington and Concord, his army fought on the open plains. He barely escaped with 9,000 men, cannon, and provisions.

General Howe offered to discuss peace terms with Franklin and Adams. They traveled to Staten Island to talk. But the peace talks collapsed, with neither side willing to negotiate or concede defeat.

The focus on war meant that no one was thinking about decorating his or her homes. Instead, they were preparing in case they might need to evacuate. No one wanted upholstered chairs or padded coach seats. Their minds were on the approaching British army. To survive, Betsy Ross may have made flags to support herself.

The war was going badly for George Washington. The British had chased him out of New York and New Jersey. They were right behind his army, heading towards Philadelphia. The volunteer army was falling apart. On November 30, two thousand men left; their enlistment time was up. The rest could leave on January 1—Betsy Ross's twenty-fifth birthday.

The Rules of War

Warfare in the eighteenth century was fought by certain rules. Armies drew up in long rows out in the open. The troops marched towards their enemy in straight columns, firing and reloading as fast as they could. The goal was to make the enemy move from its position, not to kill a lot of men. Of course, without cover, the chances of being killed or wounded were pretty high.

The British did not like the way the Minutemen fired at them from behind bushes, trees, and fences as the Redcoats retreated from Lexington and Concord. Sniper fire was considered against the rules. Washington, who played by the rules in New York, lost badly. He soon learned to change his tactics.

Washington was desperate. He wrote on December 18, 1776, "I think the game is pretty near up."[48] He needed to raise morale, and he needed foreign backing. For either, he had to win a battle. His banker friend, Robert Morris, helped obtain funds for a new campaign. In a desperate measure, Washington planned to cross the Delaware River and attack the Hessians at Trenton, New Jersey. December 26, 1776, the day after Christmas drinking and celebrating, was the date.

The ice-clogged Delaware River would have been uncrossable except for a special boat. Sixty-foot-long, eight-foot-wide Durham boats carried 2,400 men and their supplies—50 men at a time—across the river. Few of the men had overcoats for the bitter snowstorm and the nine-mile walk to Trenton.

"It will be a terrible night for the soldiers who have no shoes," one of Washington's officers wrote. "Some of them tied old rags around their feet, but I have not heard a man complain."[49]

Washington was determined. "Tell General Sullivan to use the bayonet," Washington said when informed wet muskets would not fire. "I am resolved to take Trenton."[50]

His plan worked. The Hessians were completely surprised. By 9:00 A.M., Washington's troops had taken almost a thousand prisoners, a thousand muskets, and several cannons. Only two Americans died. "This is a glorious day for our country," Washington said.[51]

The British thought differently. "All our hopes were blasted by that unhappy affair at Trenton," Lord George Germain told Parliament.[52]

Test Your Knowledge

1 In the initial voting, which two colonies opposed declaring independence?

a. New York and New Jersey.

b. Pennsylvania and North Carolina.

c. Georgia and Delaware.

d. Virginia and Rhode Island.

2 When the final vote was taken, one colony did not vote for independence. Which one?

a. New York.

b. North Carolina.

c. Pennsylvania.

d. Delaware.

3 What happened on July 4, 1776?

a. The colonies voted to declare their independence from Britain.

b. The delegates signed the Declaration of Independence.

c. The delegates approved the Declaration of Independence.

d. The Declaration of Independence was read aloud throughout the colonies.

4 Who signed the Declaration of Independence?

a. Only Thomas Jefferson, since he was its author.

b. Only John Hancock, since he was the president of the Continental Congress.

c. One delegate from each colony.

d. All of the delegates to the Continental Congress.

5 On December 26, 1776, Washington and his troops made a desperate attack on Hessian troops stationed in what town?

a. Philadelphia.

b. New York.

c. Trenton.

d. Yorktown.

ANSWERS: 1. b; 2. a; 3. c; 4. d; 5. c

OUR RIGHTS AND OUR LIBERTIES

8

Philadelphia Is Captured

After the victory at Trenton, Washington paraded Hessian prisoners through Philadelphia's streets. Betsy and crowds of people watched the enemy march down the streets.

"The old women howled dreadfully and wanted to throttle us all because we had come to America to rob them of their freedom," wrote one Hessian.[53]

Four days later, Washington marched to Princeton, New Jersey, and won a second battle against Lord Cornwallis. Practically overnight, Washington was a hero. His army swelled to 10,000. Men joined out of admiration for his accomplishments and for the 20 dollars and 100 acres of land offered for staying until the war was over.

Still, the Continental Army was hardly a threat to the most feared army in the world. General Howe could have ended the whole conflict with a quick strike against Washington's forces, but he relaxed in New York, preferring city life and a new girlfriend.

In Philadelphia, winter was hard on everyone. Betsy Ross wore a bonnet and mittens over her gray dress to keep warm inside her house. Firewood and food was scarce. Betsy's upholstery business dwindled down to a single assignment: making flags for America's navy. With the Delaware River frozen, the privateers—who had been authorized by Congress to roam the seas looking for British ships to rob—were stuck in Philadelphia. This included Captain Joseph Ashburn, who had once been Betsy's boyfriend. Betsy's brother-in-law, William Donaldson, had served with Joseph on the same ship. He re-introduced Betsy and Joseph Ashburn to each other.

Short and muscular, Ashburn had been a sailor most his life. When he was 21 years old, his aunt gave him command of her ship, the *Swallow*. With it, he sailed to the West Indies for sugar, rum, molasses, spices, and tobacco. When the war began, he became a privateer. He also supplied two forts that guarded Philadelphia's port.

The only record of Betsy Ross's flagmaking was dated May 1777. It reads, "State Navy Board, May 1777. An order on William Webb to Elizabeth Ross, for fourteen pounds, twelve shillings, two pence for making ships colors [flags]."[54]

A NEW MARRIAGE

On June 15, 1777, Joseph Ashburn and Betsy Ross were married. This time, Betsy didn't sneak off to another city. Her friends and sister who had helped with her elopement were present at the Old Swede's Church in Philadelphia.

The newlyweds lived at the Ross home on Arch Street. In colonial days, anything women owned became the property of their husbands, so Ashburn got a house and a business along with a new wife.

In June 1777, Congress passed a resolution calling for the creation of a new national flag. It was to have 13 alternating red and white stripes, with 13 white stars on a blue background.

Coincidentally, the day before the couple married, the Congress passed a resolution officially describing the new national flag: "That the Flag of the united states be 13 stripes alternate red and white, that the Union be 13 stars white in a blue field representing a new constellation."[55] It sounded a lot like Betsy Ross's flag.

During the next two months, the Ashburns saw two celebrations in the city. On July 8, Philadelphia marked the first anniversary of the Declaration of Independence with ringing bells and rattling drums. Ships on the river flew red, white, and blue flags.

The next celebration was more ominous. In August 1777, General Howe started towards Philadelphia with 267 ships, carrying 15,000 men and equipment. Washington marched his army through Philadelphia on the way to meet Howe. Betsy and her husband didn't see a very polished army on that August 24. The men had no matching uniforms. The only thing they all wore was some greenery in their hats.

John Adams wasn't impressed. "Our soldiers have not quite the air of soldiers," he wrote his wife. "They don't step exactly in time. They don't hold up their heads quite erect nor turn out their toes exactly as they ought."[56]

Washington engaged the British at the Battle of Brandywine on September 11, just 25 miles from Philadelphia. It didn't turn out well. About 1,200 colonials were killed, wounded, or taken prisoner.

Howe had 583 casualties. The British advanced on Philadelphia.

Answering Washington's call for more men, John Claypoole joined on September 13, 1777, and was commissioned a Second Lieutenant. He would later become important in Betsy's life.

For two weeks, the armies skirmished in the countryside around Philadelphia, attacking and retreating. Philadelphians panicked. About two-thirds of the population loaded their belongings into wagons, carts, and boats. They buried their valuables. The Continental Congress fled. The State House bell (later called the Liberty Bell) was taken down and hidden to prevent the British from melting it down for bullets.

Joseph Ashburn, knowing that he would be imprisoned for his privateering if the British found him, left Philadelphia. Betsy decided to remain at their business and home.

On September 25, 1777, the British marched into town, crossing Arch Street near Betsy's home. Tory supporters lined the streets, cheering. The noise of drums and fifes playing, the clatter of animal hooves, and the thud of marching feet were frightening for the Patriots, even from behind closed doors and windows.

Franklin was in Paris, negotiating for French aid when a Frenchman told Franklin that Howe had taken Philadelphia. "I beg your pardon, Sir," Franklin replied, "Philadelphia has taken Howe."[57]

From the air, the two armies would have looked like a doughnut. British forces were concentrated in the center, which was Philadelphia; the Continental Army's forces surrounded it.

On October 4, 1777, Washington attacked a British outpost at Germantown, a short distance from Philadelphia. Though he lost, the battle again showed foreign countries that the Continentals could fight.

British soldiers took over any of the 5,550 homes in Philadelphia that suited them. British officers claimed the State House; soldiers camped out on its yard. A cavalry troop stayed in Carpenters' Hall. They used its weather vane for target practice. Soldiers burned furniture, even church pews, for heat.

One captain settled into Ben Franklin's house. The prize trophy, William Penn's mansion, was reserved for General Howe and his New York girlfriend. Betsy's small house was too insignificant to be occupied.

Had Howe helped General John Burgoyne cut New England off from the other colonies, Burgoyne might not have lost at Saratoga and the war's outcome might have been different. Instead, Howe spent the winter in Philadelphia, attending balls and concerts.

Washington wintered in Valley Forge. There, a few miles from Philadelphia, colonials thought hell had frozen over. Their only shelter came from small cabins the soldiers had quickly built, with straw and earth roofs and earthen floors. Paper dipped in hog fat let in light. The soldiers ate cakes made from flour, salt, and water for every meal. Some had only rags to wrap around their feet.

An Army Without a Flag

The navy used flags to identify their ships. John Paul Jones forced a French admiral to exchange salutes on February 14, 1778. This was the first formal recognition of the American flag by a foreign power.

But for all the talk of a national flag, Washington's troops never received one. Three years after the war ended, the artillery was finally authorized to carry a national flag.

"Their feet and legs froze until they became black," the Frenchman Lafayette wrote, "and it was often necessary to amputate them."[58]

STRUGGLE FOR SURVIVAL

In Philadelphia, Patriots struggled to survive. Until the British captured two colonial-held forts and opened the Delaware River, material was in short supply. The best Betsy could do was sew dresses for Loyalist ladies and mend British uniforms. The Redcoats called her "Little Rebel."[59]

Impressed after Washington's efforts and Burgoyne's defeat at Saratoga, the French agreed to aid the Americans. Fearing that the French would trap British troops at Philadelphia, King George III ordered Howe out of Philadelphia and back to New York.

The British threw one gigantic farewell party in May. Philadelphians were horrified as Tory sympathizers and soldiers floated down the Delaware in decorated barges. Guns of warships fired salutes; bands played "God Save the King." Silk flowers were tied to tree branches, and 300 candles decorated the festivities. Some people dressed up as knights and pretended to have a medieval joust.

Finally, on June 18, 1778, the British ships sailed away in the night, and the army marched out in a twelve-mile-long caravan of soldiers, guns, and baggage. Philadelphia was rid of the British. The bad news for Betsy was that Philadelphia would be slow to recover from the British occupation. The British still blocked the Delaware River and prevented supplies from coming to Philadelphia. Food and firewood were scarce. A pound of butter that had cost 13 cents in 1775 now cost 15 dollars.

But there was good news for Betsy, as well. Her husband, Joseph Ashburn, was safe. He had hidden his ship in tiny New Jersey inlets. With the British gone, he returned home. For the next year, Ashburn continued his privateering adventures between Philadelphia and the West Indies. He was with Betsy when their daughter Lucilla, nicknamed "Zilla," was born on September 15, 1779.

Ashburn left the aging *Swallow* for a position on the *Patty* as first mate. In early October 1780, the *Patty* sailed down the Delaware and out of sight. Ashburn's trips to the West Indies normally took six weeks. Betsy hoped that he would return before the birth of their second child in February.

Historic records show that Ross sewed flags for ships during the Revolutionary War, but there is no specific evidence proving that she was commissioned to create the first American flag.

But he did not return, and Betsy heard no news of his whereabouts. She gave birth to their second daughter, Eliza, on February 25, 1781.

Betsy finally learned of her husband's fate from a childhood friend, John Claypoole. Because Claypoole's wounds from the Battle of Germantown prevented him from continuing in the army, he, too, had turned to privateering. Claypoole had sailed to France on the *Luzerne* and was returning with cannons, gunpowder, guns, and cloth in April 1881, when the ship was captured.

The crew was imprisoned in Limerick, Ireland, and then marched 72 miles to a British prison ship in Cork. It headed to Plymouth, England, and the Old Mill Prison. Claypoole joined 300 American prisoners jailed there. Among them was Betsy's husband, Joseph Ashburn, who had been there for a year. The horrible conditions, the lack of medicine, food, and water weakened Ashburn.

A November newspaper, smuggled into the prison inside a loaf of bread, announced that Cornwallis had surrendered at Yorktown, Virginia, on October 17, 1781. The American and French forces had killed half of the British troops in America in the battle.

In London, Lord North had cried, "Oh God, it is all over."[60] The Old Mill prisoners, including Claypoole and Ashburn, cheered. They hoped that they would be released. Unfortunately, Ashburn never saw freedom.

Claypoole wrote in his journal, "In the night of the 3rd of March [1782] Mr. Joseph Ashburn departed this life after an illness of about a week."[61]

That was the sad news Claypoole had to deliver when he knocked on Betsy's door in August 1782. She was 31 years old, the mother of two young daughters, and a widow for the second time.

Test Your Knowledge

1. During the harsh winter of 1777, Betsy's upholstery business dwindled to a single assignment. What was it?
   a. Sewing uniforms for the Continental Army.
   b. Sewing a flag to fly over the State House.
   c. Making flags for American ships.
   d. Sewing drapes for the windows at Carpenters' Hall.

2. What was the profession of Betsy Ross's second husband, Joseph Ashburn?
   a. He was a sailor.
   b. He was an upholsterer.
   c. He was a carpenter.
   d. He was a farmer.

3. What tragic event happened in Philadelphia in September 1777?
   a. Benjamin Franklin was murdered.
   b. British troops marched in and occupied the city.
   c. Vandals burned the State House while the Congress was in session.
   d. A yellow fever epidemic killed thousands of people.

4 Why did Betsy Ross sew dresses for Loyalist women and mend British uniforms?

a. Her husband was a Loyalist.
b. She hoped to spy on the British and gain information about their plans.
c. It was the only work she could find when British troops occupied Philadelphia.
d. She wanted to perfect her skills before working for Patriots.

5 What happened to Joseph Ashburn?

a. He died in a British prison.
b. His ship sank and none of the crew survived.
c. He continued his privateering during the war, then returned home to Philadelphia when the war ended.
d. He died at Valley Forge during the harsh winter.

ANSWERS: 1. c; 2. a; 3. b; 4. c; 5. a

OUR RIGHTS AND OUR LIBERTIES

9

War Ends

John Claypoole had known Betsy Ross when they were children. He was a Quaker, and his sisters had gone to school with Betsy. Over time, John and Betsy renewed their friendship. Betsy had just lost a husband who was a sailor. Getting involved with another one seemed foolish. Jobs on land just weren't appealing to John. Two months after he returned home, John Claypoole shipped out to sea again.

But romance gradually developed between them. By May 8, 1783, he gave up the sea for Betsy. Betsy Griscom Ross Ashburn because Betsy Griscom Ross Ashburn Claypoole. They were married in the beautiful Christ Church that she and John Ross had attended several years before.

Just like Joseph Ashburn before him, John inherited Betsy's upholstery business and home. Besides the delicate fancy work Betsy was so good at creating, the couple began to make tents, camp chairs, and cots for the army. They made mattresses, tables, and stools for ships. Having worked in his family's tannery, John could upholster with leather.

Technically, because she had married a Quaker man, Betsy could have returned to the Society of Friends. But she did not. The Claypooles rode right past the Quaker Meeting House on Arch Street on their way to the Free Quakers Meeting House. John and Betsy fit right in with the 200 people who called themselves "Free Quakers" or "Fighting Quakers." They held many Quaker beliefs, but they also had supported the war, either with their money or by joining the army. Betsy attended meetings with the Free Quakers for many years. She was one of only two remaining members left when the Meeting House was permanently closed.

The peace treaty between England and the colonies was signed on September 3, 1783, two years after Cornwallis's surrender at Yorktown. John Adams and Benjamin Franklin were among those in Paris who worked out the terms. England admitted that the colonies were independent. The new nation was bordered by Canada, the Mississippi River, and the new Spanish possessions of what we now know as Florida and parts of Alabama and Mississippi.

Philadelphia bustled with life again. Ships from many countries sailed into its port. Betsy had plenty of fabrics and cloth to make her upholstery shop successful.

The family increased when Clarissa Sidney Claypoole was born on April 3, 1785. Another daughter, Susan, was born on November 15, 1786. The Claypooles needed more room than Betsy's house on Arch Street had. Fortunately, the home of Betsy's great-grandfather, Andrew Griscom, was available, and they moved into it.

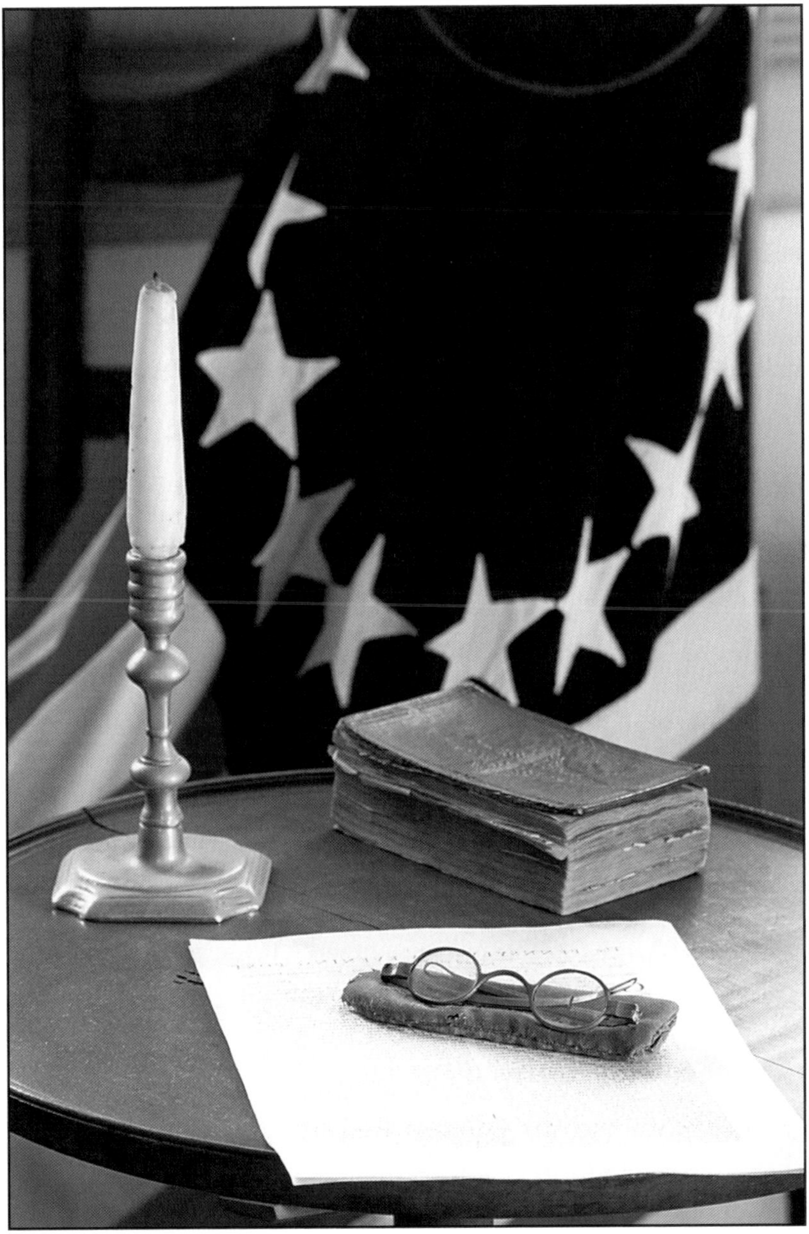

Artifacts from the Betsy Ross House prove that Ross was a successful businesswoman who sold many American flags during the early part of the nineteenth century.

Betsy and John had three more daughters: Rachel, Jane, and Harriet. Jane and Rachel grew to adulthood and had families of their own. Harriet died as a baby.

NEW RULES OF GOVERNMENT

Unfortunately, becoming independent of England did not necessarily mean that the colonies had come together as a nation. The colonies, now known as states, still thought of themselves as completely independent and quite separate from one another. If the new country was to survive, new rules of government had to be created.

John Hancock, who had become the governor of Massachusetts, said, "How to strengthen and improve the Union so as to render it completely adequate, demands the immediate attention of the states."[62]

Once again, delegates traveled to Philadelphia. Once again, the great men of the country sat down together. This time, they discussed how to make a strong government but protect the rights of individual states. A total of 55 delegates walked Philadelphia's streets from May to mid-September. Benjamin Franklin, now 81 years old, was there, along with seven other signers of the Declaration of Independence and

21 war veterans. Robert Morris, of Betsy's flag committee, nominated George Washington to preside over their convention.

The chief debates concerned how individual states would be represented in the new government. The small states wanted every state to have just one vote, regardless of population. The states with large populations wanted votes to be based on the number of people in each state. Neither side would change its position. George Washington and his friend Robert Morris were "Much dejected . . . and at this alarming crisis, a dissolution of the Convention was hourly to be expected," one delegate reported.[63]

But a compromise changed everything. Roger Sherman, a Connecticut delegate, proposed that one part of Congress be based on population (today's House of Representatives) and another part of Congress be created where all states had an equal number of votes (today's Senate). The crisis was over.

The states had won their independence and created a new form of government. The next thing the new country needed was a leader. George Washington was the logical choice to be the country's first president. The presidential electors unanimously gave him the job in March 1789. A crowd of 20,000—nearly all of Philadelphia's 28,000 residents—gave Washington a hero's welcome as he traveled to New York City to be sworn in as president.

The Claypooles may have been in the crowd when Washington departed, but they did not see him take the oath of office in New York City, wearing his sword, white silk stockings, and silver shoe buckles. However, in November 1790, the new American government was moved to Philadelphia, and remained there for ten years. Washington was as recognizable as Ben Franklin on Philadelphia streets. The country's first president rode in a fancy coach drawn by six matched horses.

John Claypoole took a government job at the custom's house while Betsy continued to run her shop. Government offices needed plenty of drapes and upholstered furniture. Meanwhile, in 1791 and 1792, Vermont and Kentucky became states, adding two more stripes and stars to the flag design.

The French Revolution in 1792 upset Americans. During the so-called "Reign of Terror"—the violent regime that marked the beginning of revolution in France—nearly 2,800 people were beheaded in Paris.

Some had fought with the American colonists during the Revolutionary War.

For this reason, Americans were divided—some feeling that the revolutionaries in France had earned America's support, while others felt that the violence in France was to be criticized, not supported. Washington was determined to keep his new country out of the troubles of other nations. Some agreed with him; others violently objected. John Adams later wrote about "the terrorism," and how "ten thousand people in the streets of Philadelphia . . . threatened to drag Washington out of his house."[64] Nevertheless, Washington was unanimously elected to a second term.

OUTBREAK IN PHILADELPHIA

In August 1793, an epidemic of yellow fever hit Philadelphia. Its high fever, skin blisters, black vomit, and yellow coloration of the skin could kill within 12 hours. Doctors didn't yet know that mosquitoes that bred in the stagnant water around the city carried the disease. They thought it was caused by something in the air and ordered gunpowder burned and cannons fired every hour while they bled victims of "excess" blood for good measure. Those brave enough to go outside their homes chewed garlic and wet their clothes with vinegar—remedies thought to prevent the disease. The government and half the population, including George and Martha Washington, fled the city until cold weather lessened the epidemic. Businesses closed; newspapers stopped publishing. Philadelphia almost became a ghost town.

People died all around Betsy and her family. Fortunately, Betsy, John, and their children survived, but Betsy's parents and sister were among the 5,000 who did not.

The country was shocked on September 19, 1796, when the Philadelphia *Daily American Advertiser* published Washington's letter "To the PEOPLE of the United States/Friends and fellow citizens."[65] In it, Washington announced that he would not run for a third term. The country's second president was John Adams. On March 4, 1797, he defeated Thomas Jefferson, who became vice president.

FINAL YEARS

In 1812, Betsy's flagmaking business boomed. With the United States at war with Britain again, ships needed American flags to identify themselves. She did not, however, make the large flag that inspired Francis Scott Key to write "The Star Spangled Banner" during a battle at Fort McHenry. That job went to Mary Pickersgill in Baltimore, Maryland.

Eventually, John Claypoole's health weakened from his war injuries and months in prison. He could no longer work at the customs house. Betsy became the main money earner with her upholstery business. Finally, John Claypoole, Betsy's husband of 34 years, died on August 3, 1817.

The Star-Spangled Banner

The flag that inspired Francis Scott Key's poem, whose words would eventually became the national anthem, was 30 feet by 42 feet large. It was made out of 1,200 feet of wool. The 15 stars were two feet across from point to point. The stripes were two feet wide. Its linen backing had been sewn to the flag with 1,700,000 stitches. Mrs. Mary Pickersgill of Baltimore was paid $405.90 for making it.

It flew over Fort McHenry at the harbor of Baltimore. Major George Armistead wanted a flag "so large that the British will have no difficulty seeing it from a distance."

Betsy could have retired then, at age 65, but she did not. She continued to work for another ten years, using her needles and thread.

For a while, it seemed that the American flag's shape and design would be ruined, as more states were admitted into the union. But Betsy lived to see the 1818 Flag Act limit the stripes at 13 and establish a star for each new state.

Finally, in 1827, at age 75, Betsy turned her shop over to her daughter, Clarissa, and her niece, Margaret Boggs. She closed her shop and went to live first with her daughter, Susan, and Susan's husband, and then with Jane and her husband, Caleb Canby. Their son, William Canby, would tell the story of his grandmother and the first flag.

By 1834, Betsy was one of only two surviving members of the Free Quakers. Its membership had once included Nathanael Green, another Revolutionary War hero. But with only Betsy and another member left, the Society of Free Quakers closed its doors for the last time.

In her old age, Betsy lost her eyesight. She died in her sleep at the home of her daughter, Jane, on January 30, 1836, at the age of 84. She was buried in the cemetery of the Society of Free Quakers and then was moved two more times until she was laid to rest in the courtyard adjacent to her home. She was buried next to her husband, John Claypoole.

In 1870, her grandson, William Canby, publicized his grandmother's story after interviewing his mother and aunts about their recollections. He presented his version of the first American flag to the Pennsylvania Historical Society.

Test Your Knowledge

1 Before he married Betsy Ross, what did John Claypoole do?

a. He was an upholsterer.

b. He was a doctor.

c. He was a spy.

d. He was a sailor.

2 What made the "Free Quakers" unique?

a. They held many Quaker beliefs, but also supported the Revolutionary War.

b. They believed that women should be free to marry as they wished, to own and operate their own businesses, and to manage property.

c. They supported the idea of an independent, self-governing Quaker state.

d. They hoped to bring an end to slavery.

3 What was the second capital of the United States?

a. New York.

b. Philadelphia.

c. Washington, D.C.

d. Williamsburg, Virginia.

4 Why was 1812 a good year for Betsy Ross's business?

a. The economy was booming, and many Philadelphians could afford fine upholstered goods.
b. War with Britain meant that there was a demand for flags.
c. More states were added to the United States, so new flags needed to be created.
d. None of the above.

5 How did the Flag Act of 1818 affect the design of the American flag?

a. It limited the number of stripes to 13.
b. It changed the flag's colors to red, white, and blue.
c. It removed two stars and added two stripes.
d. It changed the color of the stars from blue to white.

ANSWERS: 1. d; 2. a; 3. b; 4. b; 5. a

10

OUR RIGHTS AND OUR LIBERTIES

Two Different Views

The general public and historians have two different ideas about Betsy Ross and the making of the country's first flag. Almost every child learns that Betsy Ross sewed the first flag, being told a story much like the one that Betsy's grandson told. Historians have looked for evidence in sources of the past to prove that this story is actually true. They have not found any.

Historians point out that there is no record of a congressional committee appointed to design a flag, or that a committee of George Washington, Robert Morris, and George Ross existed at all. Betsy's supporters are not bothered by that. They say that the committee was secret and that the congressional records were often inaccurate.

Historians point out that the Continental Congress did not vote on an "official" flag until one year after Betsy supposedly made it. Even then, the notes of the meeting did not describe what the flag should look like, except that it should have horizontal stripes.

Betsy's supporters point out that the Congress was busy with other items of business—like managing a war, keeping an army together, and discussing how to make a new country. Voting on the design of a flag may not have been high on their list of tasks to complete.

Betsy's story includes three important men. It is true, Betsy supporters say, that George Washington was in Philadelphia from May 23 to June 5, the time period in which the "secret committee" supposedly came to Betsy's house. But historians point out that, by this

The story of Betsy Ross as creator of the nation's first flag has become legendary, even without strong historical evidence to support it.

time, Washington was the commander-in-chief of the Continental Army. He had other terrible problems to consider. For one thing, he knew that the British were preparing to attack New York. That would have been foremost on his mind during this time. He was constantly worried about getting his men enough supplies and money.

According to the legend, it was Washington who presented the flag to the Congress. As a critical figure in the struggle for independence, Washington's words and actions were closely watched and recorded. Historians point out, again, that there is no record of Washington saying anything to the Congress about a new flag.

Betsy's story includes Robert Morris. He was an important man, too. He was Washington's financier, finding money to keep the war going. More importantly, as a delegate for Pennsylvania, he was against breaking away from England. In July 1776, he hoped that there could be an end to the hostilities without declaring independence. He purposely stayed away while the delegates voted for independence, allowing Pennsylvania's pro-independence delegates to be in the majority and vote for breaking away from England.

Why would he be part of a committee to make up a flag for a new nation he hoped would never be created? It would make more sense for him to have been on such a committee after the Declaration of Independence was signed. By that time, he was willing to pledge his support of the decision for independence.

George Ross was the third member of Betsy's secret committee. Betsy's supporters point out that he was related to her first husband and probably knew of her sewing skills. But Ross was elected to Congress on July 20, 1776. The committee supposedly met with Betsy in either May or June, four to eight weeks before he was a member of the Congress. He joined the group and signed the Declaration of Independence on August 2, although he was not a member when Congress voted for independence. An interesting question would be why would Congress ask a non-member to serve on one of its committees?

MORE QUESTIONS

The bigger question skeptics ask concerns the flag-making project itself. Betsy's story takes place in May or June of 1776. The delegates were still so divided about declaring independence in June that they went home after Richard Lee's motion for independence. Having not yet made up their minds on declaring independence, why would the delegates appoint a committee to design a flag for an independent nation?

Betsy supporters point to the receipt made out to Betsy for making "colours" for ships in 1777. Skeptics point out that there is no description of the design she sewed and that there is no other receipt before that time paying her for her efforts.

Skeptics also wonder how accurate Betsy's story could be since it is based on her grandson's recollections of something he heard when he was 11 years old from a grandmother who was 84 years old. Statements that other people gave about the truth of the story were from other relatives of advanced years, as well. William Canby told the story in 1870, 94 years after

The Other First Flagmaker

Francis Hopkinson was another person who claimed to have designed the official flag of the United States. He was notable for other things, as well. He was the first student to enroll at the University of Pennsylvania. He signed the Declaration of Independence. He helped design other items, including the Great Seal of the United States and the seal for the state of New Jersey.

In 1780, he billed the Congress, asking for today's equivalent of 24 dollars' worth of wine for designing the first national flag. Congress would not honor his request, claiming that he already worked for the government as a member of the Continental Navy Board and shouldn't charge for these things. Another reason Congress refused to pay him was that it noted that the design had not been Hopkinson's, but that others had contributed to it, as well.

Betsy supposedly picked up the scissors to snip a five-pointed star for General Washington.

Perhaps the strongest point those who believe Betsy sewed the first flag emphasize is her character. No skeptic can question that. Betsy was raised as a Quaker. Quakers were sincere, religious people who built their lives on honesty and truth. In the first place, it would simply be against all she believed to "stretch the truth" and make up a tall tale. Secondly, her story didn't include unknown politicians. Betsy's account centers on the most respected individual in the country, George Washington, and two signers of one of the most important documents in the world.

We have more evidence about her character. She did stand up for what was important. She left all that was important to her to marry John Ross. She did, after all, support the Patriot cause when many living in Philadelphia supported the British or refused to take a stand. Those who don't believe the Betsy story don't disagree with what is known of Betsy Ross's character.

In the end, whether Canby's story is myth or truth isn't very important. Betsy Griscom Ross Ashburn Claypoole lived during one of the most exciting times in our nation's history. She experienced the beginning of the revolution and its end. She was busy sewing flags and upholstering furniture when colonial delegates declared their independence and created a constitution that works today. The people we now revere as "founding fathers" of our country walked the same streets she did. George Washington, John Adams, Thomas Jefferson, James Madison, James Monroe, John Quincy Adams, and Andrew Jackson served as presidents during her lifetime. A total of 24 states joined the Union and added their stars to the flag while she was alive. Whether she made one flag or a thousand, whether she made the first or copies after it was created, seems unimportant. The country the Stars and Stripes represents endures. And its spirit of independence, which Betsy demonstrated so well throughout her life, lives on in millions of Americans today.

Test Your Knowledge

1. What was the source of the story that Betsy Ross designed the first American flag?
   a. Diaries kept by George Washington.
   b. Receipts in Betsy Ross's shop showing that a flag had been designed for the Continental Congress.
   c. Records from meetings of the Continental Congress.
   d. Memories from Betsy Ross's family, publicized by her grandson.

2. Why do historians criticize the legend that George Washington was part of the "secret committee"?
   a. They say that he was not in Philadelphia at the time.
   b. They say that he would have used a flagmaker from Virginia.
   c. They say that, as commander-in-chief of the Continental Army, his focus would have been on the war, not creating a flag.
   d. They say that he felt that American troops should not carry flags into battle.

3. Why does Robert Morris's legendary role in the flag design seem unlikely?
   a. At the time, he was not in favor of independence from Britain.
   b. At the time, he was in France attempting to gain French support for the American cause.
   c. He did not like the Ross family and would not have asked Betsy Ross to be the flag's designer.
   d. He did not like Washington and would never have served on a committee with him.

4 Why was George Ross probably not a member of the secret committee?

a. As Betsy Ross's husband, it would have been a conflict of interest for him to commission his own wife for such an important task.

b. He was busy working with Thomas Jefferson on the draft of the Declaration of Independence, and would not have had time to serve on any other committees.

c. He was not yet a member of the Continental Congress when the committee supposedly asked Betsy Ross to create the flag.

d. He was a Loyalist and fled the country after the war ended.

5 What aspect of Betsy Ross's life suggests that the legend could be true?

a. She was an excellent seamstress.

b. She was an honest, sincere woman who did not tell lies.

c. Her neighbors called her "The Flag Lady."

d. She was a close friend of George Washington's and had designed the uniform worn by the soldiers in the Continental Army.

ANSWERS: 1. d; 2. c; 3. a; 4. c; 5. b

1751 Betsy Griscom is born on January 1 in West Jersey, Pennsylvania.

1754 Griscom family moves to Philadelphia.

1764 Betsy's schooling ends.

1765 Betsy becomes an upholstery apprentice.

1773 Betsy marries John Ross.

1776 John Ross dies in an explosion on January 21; George Washington asks Betsy Ross to make a flag in June.

1777 Betsy's flag becomes the official flag of the United States; Betsy marries Joseph Ashburn.

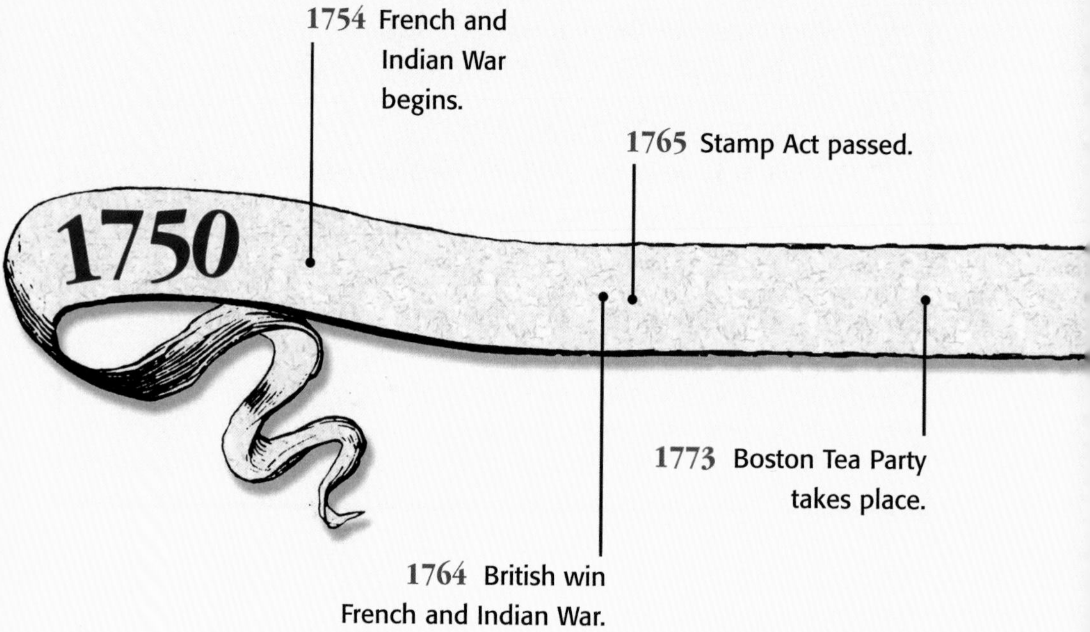
1750
1754 French and Indian War begins.
1765 Stamp Act passed.
1773 Boston Tea Party takes place.
1764 British win French and Indian War.

1779 Daughter Lucilla is born on September 15.

1781 Daughter Eliza is born on February 25.

1782 Joseph Ashburn dies in an English prison.

1783 Betsy marries John Claypoole on May 8.

1785 Daughter Clarissa Sidney is born on April 3.

1786 Daughter Susan is born on November 15.

1790 Philadelphia becomes the nation's capital.

1795 Daughter Harriet is born on December 20.

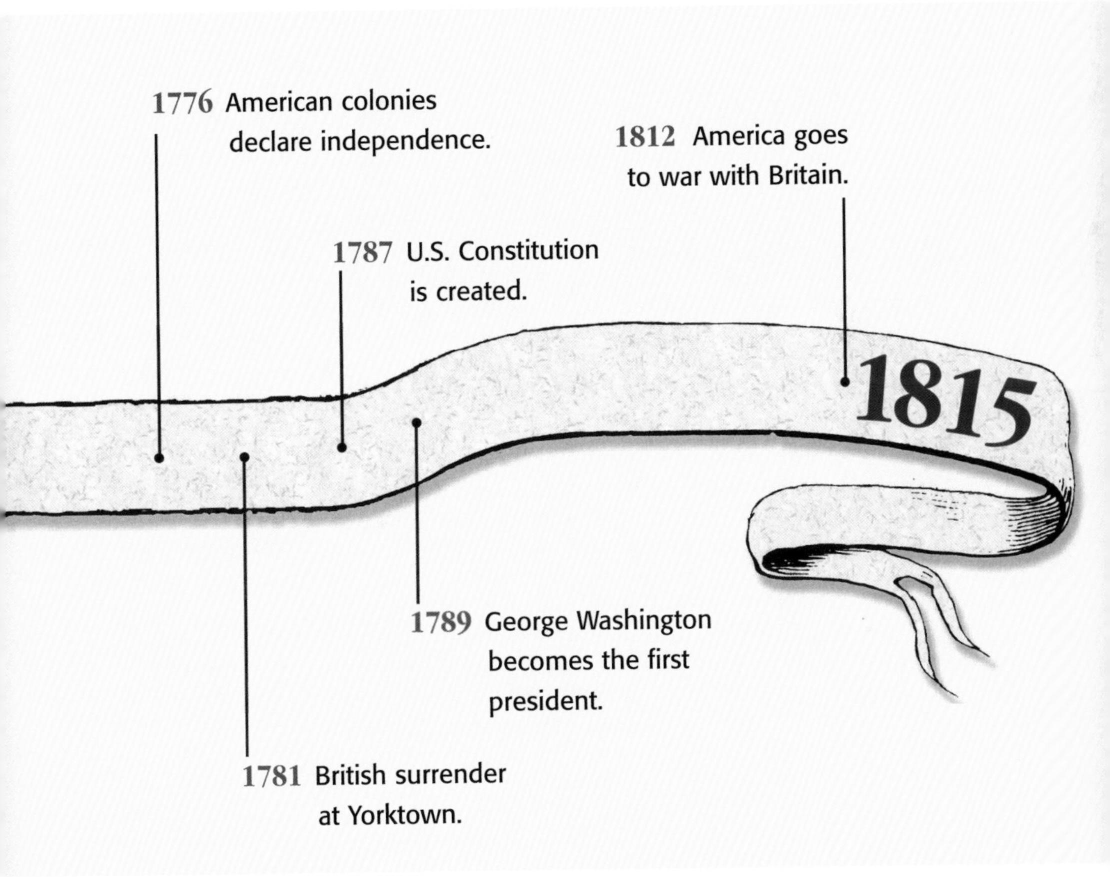
1776 American colonies declare independence.
1812 America goes to war with Britain.
1787 U.S. Constitution is created.
1815
1789 George Washington becomes the first president.
1781 British surrender at Yorktown.

Chronology

1800 Congress moves capital from Philadelphia to Washington, D.C.

1812 America goes to war with Britain.

1816 John Claypoole dies on August 3.

1827 Betsy retires and lives with her daughters.

1836 Betsy dies on January 30.

1870 Betsy's grandson, William Canby, tells her story.

Notes

CHAPTER 1:
The Legend of Betsy Ross

1 Peter and Connie Roop, *Betsy Ross* (New York: Scholastic, 2001), 60.

CHAPTER 2:
Quaker Family Life

2 Kieran Doherty, *William Penn Quaker Colonist* (Brookfield, Conn.: Millbrook Press, 1998), 99.

3 Ibid., 102.

4 Jean Kinney Williams, *The Quakers* (New York: Franklin Watt, 1998), 61.

CHAPTER 3:
Growing Up with the Colonies

5 J. William Frost, *The Quaker Family in Colonial America* (New York: St. Martin's Press, 1973), 112.

6 Ibid.

7 Ibid., 114.

8 Ibid., 123.

9 Ibid., 95.

10 Alice Dickinson, *The Stamp Act* (New York: Franklin Watts, 1970), 26.

CHAPTER 4:
A Rebellion in the Colonies

11 Ibid., 4.

12 Frost, 173.

13 Ibid.

14 Roop, 37.

15 Ibid.

16 Russell F. Weigley, *Philadelphia: A 300-Year History* (New York: W.W. Norton, 1982), 118.

17 Ibid.

18 Russell Freedman, *Give Me Liberty!* (New York: Holiday House, 2000), 2.

19 Steven C. Bullock, *The American Revolution: A History in Documents* (Oxford, U.K.: Oxford University Press, 2003), 37.

20 Albert Marrin, *George Washington & the Founding of a Nation* (New York: Dutton, 2001), 82.

21 Freedman, 4.

22 Marrin, 82.

23 Freedman, 25.

CHAPTER 5:
A Time of War

24 Ibid., 29.

25 Ibid., 36.

26 A.J. Langguth, *Patriots: The Men Who Started the American Revolution* (New York: Simon & Schuster, 1988), 239.

27 Freedman, 42.

28 Ibid., 43.

29 Marrin, 91.

30 Ibid., 93.

31 Langguth, 276.

32 Ibid., 278.

33 Ibid., 281.

34 Freedman, 51.

35 Langguth, 289.

Notes

CHAPTER 6:
Betsy Ross and the Founding Fathers

36 Ibid., 308.

37 Bullock, 50.

38 Freedman, 57.

39 Lora Polack Oberle, *The Declaration of Independence* (Mankato, Minn.: Bridgestone Books, 2002), 19.

40 Donald Barr Chidsey, *July 4, 1776* (New York: Crown Publishers, 1958), 41.

41 Freedman, 61.

42 Oberle, 20.

CHAPTER 7:
A New Nation

43 Chidsey, 52.

44 Ibid., 54.

45 Langguth, 360.

46 Roop, 70-71.

47 Chidsey, 105.

48 Roop, 76.

49 Christopher Collier and James Lincoln Collier, *The American Revolution: 1763–1783* (New York: Benchmark Books, 1998), 69.

50 Ibid.

51 Marrin, 132.

52 Roop, 78.

CHAPTER 8:
Philadelphia Is Captured

53 Marrin, 132.

54 Roop, 79.

55 Ibid., 80.

56 Marrin, 143.

57 Ibid., 147.

58 Ibid., 149.

59 Judith St. George, *Betsy Ross: Patriot of Philadelphia* (New York: Henry Holt, 1997), 76.

60 Collier, 83.

61 Roop, 104.

CHAPTER 9:
War Ends

62 Collier, 25.

63 Ibid., 41.

64 Marrin, 238.

65 Richard Brookhiser, *Founding Father: Rediscovering George Washington* (New York: The Free Press, 1996), 101.

Bibliography

Binns, Tristan Boyer. *The Liberty Bell.* Chicago: Heinemann Library, 2001.

Brenner, Barbara. *If You Were There in 1776.* New York: Macmillan Books for Young Readers, 1994.

Brookhiser, Richard. *Founding Father: Rediscovering George Washington.* New York: The Free Press, 1996.

Bullock, Steven C. *The American Revolution: A History in Documents.* Oxford, U.K.: Oxford University Press, 2003.

Chidsey, Donald Barr. *July 4, 1776.* New York: Crown Publishers, Inc., 1958.

Collier, Christopher and Collier, James Lincoln. *The American Revolution: 1763–1783.* New York: Benchmark Books, 1998.

Dickinson, Alice. *The Stamp Act.* New York: Franklin Watts, 1970.

Doherty, Kieran. *William Penn Quaker Colonist.* Brookfield, Conn.: The Milbrook Press, 1998.

Earle, Alice Morse. *Home Life in Colonial Days.* New York: Macmillan Company, 1898.

Fink, Sam. *The Declaration of Independence: The Words that Made America.* New York: Scholastic Inc., 2002.

Freedman, Russell. *Give Me Liberty!* New York: Holiday House, 2000.

Frost, J. William. *The Quaker Family in Colonial America.* New York: St. Martin's Press, 1973.

Harness, Cheryl. *George Washington.* Washington, D.C.: National Geographic Society, 2000.

Hinrichs, Kit and Hirasuna, Delphine. *Long May She Wave.* Berkley: Ten Speed Press, 2001.

Jefferson, Thomas. *Jefferson.* New York: The Library of America, 1984.

Bibliography

Jones, Rufus M. *The Quakers in the American Colonies.* London: Macmillan and Company, 1911.

Juden, Jane. *Betsy Ross.* Mankato, Minn.: Bridgestone Books, 2002.

Kent, Deborah. *Lexington and Concord.* New York: Children's Press, 1997.

Klingel, Cynthia and Noyed, Robert B. *The Boston Tea Party.* Chanhassen, Minn.: The Child's World, 2002.

Langguth, A.J. *Patriots: The Men Who Started the American Revolution.* New York: Simon & Schuster, 1988.

Marrin, Albert. *George Washington & the Founding of a Nation.* New York: Dutton Children's Books, 2001.

Mayer, Albert I. *The Story of Old Glory.* Chicago: Children's Press, 1970.

Miller, Susan Martins. *Betsy Ross: American Patriot.* Philadelphia: Chelsea House, 2000.

Oberle, Lora Polack. *The Declaration of Independence.* Mankato, Minn.: Bridgestone Books, 2002.

Parker, Lewis K. *The Battle of Trenton.* San Diego, Calif.: Blackbirch Press, 2002.

Parrish, Thomas. *The American Flag: The Symbol of Our Nation Throughout Its History.* New York: Simon & Schuster, 1973.

Peacock, Louise. *Crossing the Delaware.* New York: Atheneum Books for Young Readers, 1998.

Randolph, Ryan P. *Betsy Ross: The American Flag and Life in Young America.* New York: Rosen Publishing Group, 2002.

Roop, Peter and Roop, Connie. *Betsy Ross.* New York: Scholastic, Inc., 2001.

Bibliography

Schneider, Richard H. *Stars & Stripes Forever.* New York: William Morrow, 2003.

St. George, Judith. *Betsy Ross: Patriot of Philadelphia*. New York: Henry Holt, 1997.

———. *John and Abigail Adams: An American Love Story*. New York: Holiday House, 2001.

Wade, Linda R. *Early Battles of the American Revolution.* Edina, Minn.: ABDO Publishers, 2001.

———. *Final Years of the American Revolution.* Edina, Minn.: ABDO Publishers, 2001.

———. *Leaders of the American Revolution.* Edina, Minn.: ABDO Publishers, 2001.

Weigley, Russell F., ed. *Philadelphia: A 300-Year History*. New York: W.W. Norton & Company, 1982.

Williams, Jean Kinney. *The Quakers*. New York: Franklin Watts, 1998.

Yolen, Jane. *Friend: The Story of George Fox and the Quakers.* New York: The Seabury Press, 1972.

Further Reading

Bacon, Margaret H. *The Quiet Rebels: The Story of the Quakers in America.* New York: Basic Books, 1969.

Collier, Christopher and Collier, James Lincoln. *The American Revolution 1763–1783.* New York: Benchmark Books, 1998.

———. *Creating the Constitution 1787.* New York: Benchmark Books, 1999.

DeBarr, Candice M. and Bonkowske, Jack A. *Saga of the American Flag: An Illustrated History*. Tucson, Ariz.: Harbinger House, 1990.

Freedman, Russell. *Give Me Liberty!* New York: Holiday House, 2000.

Randolph, Ryan P. *Betsy Ross: The American Flag and Life in Young America.* New York: Rosen Publishing Group, 2002.

Ray, Jeffrey, ed. "Life and Liberty in Colonial Philadelphia." *Cobblestone Magazine* October (2004).

Roop, Peter and Roop, Connie. *Betsy Ross*. New York: Scholastic, Inc., 2001.

WEBSITES

Images from the Continental Congress
www.loc.gov/exhibits/jefferson/images/vc57.jpg

Independence Hall Association
www.ushistory.org

Liberty Bell
www.nps.gov/inde/liberty-bell.html

Liberty! The American Revolution
www.pbs.org/ktca/liberty

Index

Index

Picture Credits

page:

3: © Scala/Art Resource, NY
5: © CORBIS
14: © Bettmann/CORBIS
19: © Lee Snider/Photo Images/ CORBIS
29: © Bettmann/CORBIS
31: © Giraudon/Art Resource, NY
48: © Scala/Art Resource, NY
61: © Bettmann/CORBIS
64: © Bettmann/CORBIS
73: © Owaki-Kulla/CORBIS
86: © Bettmann/CORBIS
96: © Getty Images
103: © Bettmann/CORBIS
111: © Richard T. Nowtiz/ CORBIS
124: © PoodlesRock/CORBIS

Cover: © Bettmann/CORBIS

About the Author

VICKI COX is a freelance writer for magazines and newspapers. She is the author of seven biographies and an anthology titled *Rising Stars and Ozark Constellations*, which profiles people and places in the Ozarks. She has an M.S. in education, taught public school for 25 years, and has been an instructor for Drury University in Springfield, Missouri. She is past president of the Missouri Writer's Guild.